GET
STUFF
DONE

CARO HANDLEY

THUNDER BAY
P·R·E·S·S
San Diego, California

Thunder Bay Press
An imprint of Printers Row Publishing Group
10350 Barnes Canyon Road, Suite 100, San Diego, CA 92121
www.thunderbaybooks.com

Publisher: Peter Norton
Associate Publisher: Ana Parker
Publishing/Editorial Team: April Farr, Vicki Jaeger, Kelly Larsen, Stephanie Romero, Lauren Taniguchi, Kathryn C. Dalby, Carrie Davis
Editorial Team: JoAnn Padgett, Melinda Allman
Production Team: Jonathan Lopes, Rusty von Dyl

Library of Congress Cataloging-in-Publication Data is available upon request.
ISBN: 978-1-68412-847-1

Printed in the United States of America

22 21 20 19 18   1 2 3 4 5

CONTENTS

INTRODUCTION

GET STUFF DONE is everything today's woman needs, inside one cover. Easy to carry with you, fun to read and highly effective, it charts the path to success in the key areas of work, money, love and relationships.

Most of life's problems and challenges fall under the headings of love, money and work. When these areas are running smoothly and successfully, when we deal easily and happily with setbacks and feel that everything is running in harmony, then we are confident and life feels good. But if a relationship is going badly, if you're unhappy at work or if you have money worries, then it undermines confidence and leads to worry and uncertainty.

What we need when things aren't going our way is answers and solutions; a way of shifting a situation that seems stuck or making a change that points us in a new direction. That's where GET STUFF DONE comes in, with easy-to-follow steps that will address anything that isn't working in your life and lead you straight to success.

On every page you'll find exercises, tips, suggestions and advice that will help you to break old, unhelpful patterns, think in ways you've never thought before and tap your inner well of willpower and resourcefulness to help you take charge of your life. And while you can dip into any part of the book to find inspiration, ideas and encouragement, the best way to use it is to pick the area you want to work on - money, career, dating or relationships - and follow the 30 steps, one at a time. I recommend that you do one step each day, as a way of keeping up momentum and charting your progress.

When you've made the changes you want in one area of your life, look at the steps for the other three areas. Even when things are working well, you will find ideas and exercises that will enable you to make positive shifts, choose wise options and make the most of every situation.

Most of all, GET STUFF DONE is for you to enjoy. Making life work for you, bringing about the changes you want and taking charge of your life can be fun as well as productive, energizing as well as challenging.

It's time to get stuff done, and lead the life you truly want.

MONEY

We all deserve financial security, abundance and the skills and confidence to manage money in our lives. You deserve these things - and you can have them. Not one day in the future, but right now. No matter how dire your financial situation, you can turn it around and feel confident and successful with money if you really want to. Learn how to enjoy money instead of worrying about it. To avoid debt and be in control. To feel rich instead of poor.

Of course, it takes time to learn new money habits and make them part of your life. You can, however, put the stepping stones in place very easily. Once you are feeling differently about money, once you are in control and know how to handle and manage money, it will be far easier to make your new habits second nature.

To attract the money you want into your life, you need to know how to manage money, how to be generous with it, how to keep it flowing and how to treat it with respect but never fear. In this section, I will show you how, in 30 simple steps, your attitude to money and the role of money in your life can be transformed. Follow each step and choose to be successful with money and to live a life of financial ease.

"WHEN YOU UNDERVALUE WHAT YOU DO, THE WORLD WILL UNDERVALUE WHO YOU ARE."

OPRAH

STEP ONE: MONEY MATTERS

Today I want you to look at the role of money in your life. Like it or not, money is important. Everyone needs it and needs to know how to use it, manage it and bring it into their lives. Some people seem naturally brilliant with money, attracting loads of it and surrounding themselves with luxury. Others are simply comfortable with it and never worry. Then there are those who never seem to have enough, worry a lot and spend what little they do have too fast, or hang on to it so tightly that they can never enjoy what they have.

WHAT'S YOUR RELATIONSHIP WITH MONEY?

See which of the following descriptions sounds like you. Tick all those that ring true, then add any more that occur to you. You may identify with more than one:

☐ You earn plenty of money, but spend it even faster than you earn it.

☐ You make a reasonable amount and muddle through, but don't really feel on top of things financially.

☐ You sit tight on your money and agonize about every expense.

☐ You can handle the day-to-day stuff, but the bigger things such as pensions and investments are a mystery.

☐ You don't have any idea how to organize your money. You feel out of control when it comes to your finances.

☐ You're always broke and, when you feel down, spend money you don't have.

☐ You have a very low income and you're sick of struggling.

☐ You're always borrowing from friends or family, taking out loans or running up overdrafts.

☐ You have no idea how much you actually owe, but it's probably a lot.

☐ You feel ashamed of the mess you make with money and yet you're reluctant to seek help.

However many of these statements are true of you, don't feel like a failure. You're not alone! The majority of people have trouble handling money, overspend, feel that they don't have enough and worry. A great number of people overspend. And, for many people, having money troubles leads to low self-esteem and anxiety.

The good news is that these are problems that can be solved. Absolutely anyone can learn to be good with money. There's no mystery, miracle or hard-to-learn skill about it. All you need is resolve, staying power and the willingness to do things differently and pull your head out of the sand. Decide today that you're going to make money your friend, rather than your enemy. Choose financial success, rather than failure.

You can choose to be good with money right now.

STEP TWO: YOUR BELIEFS

Now I want you to examine your beliefs about money. One key thing in life that can hold us back more than anything else is our belief system. Why? Because our thoughts are based on our beliefs, and our actions are a result of our thoughts. In other words, everything we think and do stems from our beliefs. Here's an example.

Claudia believed that she didn't deserve to have a lot of money. She also believed that she would never earn more than her older sister, who had done better at school and had been considered the "clever" one in the family. As a result, Claudia took a boring job and told herself she must put up with it. She was so convinced of this that, when she was offered promotion, she turned it down. She was afraid that she wouldn't cope. Then she was offered a better job elsewhere, which she also turned down.

Claudia was determined to prove her beliefs true. It was only after she decided to change her beliefs that she took action. She found a better job, earned more and soon realized she was excellent at what she did. Within three years, she was a star in the company and was earning more than her sister.

What were Claudia's new beliefs? That she could do anything she wanted and that she was talented and deserved to be well rewarded and earn a great salary.

Root out the beliefs that hold you back.

Do you identify with any of these? Tick the ones that apply and add more of your own:

☐ I'm hopeless with money.

☐ I'll never earn much.

☐ Other people have plenty of money, not me.

☐ Money just slips through my fingers.

☐ I don't deserve to have money.

☐ Money is dirty - you can't be rich and be a good person.

☐ I'll never be in control of my money.

☐ Bills and demands are scary - I dread them.

☐ There isn't enough money to go round.

☐ I'm always afraid that my money will run out.

All these beliefs stem from a poverty mentality. The majority of people think in this "there will never be enough" way.

....

....

....

....

....

....

....

....

....

....

Now choose to let those beliefs go and to adopt some new ones. It's time to shift into abundance mentality and to welcome money into your life.

Use any of the following beliefs, plus some of your own:

☐ There's more than enough to go round.

☐ You can have lots of money and be a good person.

☐ I deserve to have a life filled with abundance.

☐ I can earn all the money I want.

☐ I respect all my bills, grateful for whatever I am paying for and knowing I can pay them easily.

☐ I manage my money well, knowing I can be generous and still have plenty left.

☐ I find it easy to control my money.

☐ I'm great with money.

☐ I choose to enjoy my money, knowing there will always be enough.

Once you have chosen your new beliefs, repeat them to yourself often and say them out loud when you can. Whenever an old, unhelpful belief pops up in your mind, just replace it instantly with a new belief. Remember that our beliefs are simply a measure of the way we see the world. We can choose our attitude and our beliefs, and by doing so encourage our life to follow the path we have chosen.

Choose to believe in abundance and feel instantly richer.

STEP THREE: SELF-ESTEEM

Today is the day for examining your self-esteem in relation to money. Self-esteem can vary in different areas of our lives. You may feel confident in and proud of your work, but self-doubting and uncertain in relationships.

How are you when it comes to money? The level of your monetary self-esteem will have a huge impact on your financial success and the way in which you deal with money matters. Put simply, self-esteem is the way you feel about yourself.

To find out what your self-esteem is really like around money, answer the following:

☐ Do you often worry about money?

☐ Do you doubt your ability to earn the amount you'd like?

☐ Do you often find yourself in debt?

☐ Does your heart sink when you think about money?

☐ Do you feel guilty when you do have money?

☐ Do you find yourself spending it as fast as you get it?

☐ Do you hide the amount of money you have?

If you ticked yes to any of these questions, your self-esteem in regard to money matters is not as high as it could be. If you answered yes to three or more, your self-esteem is definitely low.

When you have low self-esteem in relation to money, it stops you bringing money into your life, being able to enjoy it or being able to hold on to it. Either you can't earn the amount you'd like or you earn well but spend it as fast as you can so that you won't have the pleasure of having it. Or perhaps you have money, but refuse to enjoy it and treat yourself. Whatever the case, now is the time to make changes.

Here is a simple guide to raising your self-esteem:

* Treat yourself in the way that you would a good friend: with kindness and compassion, understanding and forgiveness.

* Focus on your strengths, rather than what you consider to be your faults and weaknesses.

* Nurture yourself, and help yourself to grow.

* Talk to yourself in positive ways, appreciating all your achievements.

* Cultivate self-belief by encouraging and praising yourself.

* If you are weighed down by painful, unresolved issues from your past, be willing to let them go and move on. Try to forgive everyone, including yourself. Remember that every day you have the choice between happiness and unhappiness, and that past hurts can be a source of great strength in the present.

Raising your self-esteem will benefit all areas of your life, not just your finances. Feeling good about yourself will lead to feeling in control, making better judgements and drawing more money into your life. You will also be able to stop spending money recklessly simply to cheer yourself up or comfort yourself.

Raise your self-esteem in relation to money and feel empowered.

STEP FOUR: WHERE HAS IT ALL GONE?

Today it's crunch time - time to think about where all the money you've had in your life so far has gone and whether you're happy with the choices you have made. We live in a society in which material things are very important. Most of us have a wishlist of things we'd like to own. Most of us already own a great deal. We also live in a society where spending is encouraged, whether or not we have money. We spend on goods, holidays, entertainment and gambling - to name just a few. Look around you. The things in your home are money turned into goods. Almost everything you have cost money. How much money is there in the room with you?

We choose the way we spend our money. Understanding the choices you have made and deciding whether you are happy with those choices are vital first steps to making changes.

EXERCISE

Write a list of things you have spent money on in the past three years. You might include:

* Training courses or classes.

* Material goods, such as phones, laptops or kitchen equipment, for example.

* Mortgage or rent.

* Bills.

* Clothes and shoes, make-up, accessories.

* Travel.

* Entertainment - meals out, films, shows, clubs.

* Loans and debt repayment.

* Alcohol or drugs.

....

....

....

....

....

....

....

Be totally honest when making your list. Then highlight the three areas where you spend the most. Think about how important these are to you and how you feel about your spending in these areas. Tick the box if the answer is yes to the following questions:

☐ Are you happy with the amount you have spent in each of these three categories?

☐ Are you happy with what you have to show for your spending? Are the things you paid for important, useful or a source of pleasure for you?

☐ Are these three categories the most important to you and the right priorities?

☐ What changes would you make now if you could?

The answers to these questions will give you key information about your spending patterns and the way you feel about them. You should, by now, have a clearer idea of some of the changes you want and need to make. If you've been overspending on unnecessary things, or avoiding important areas, it's time to use your money in different ways.

Investigating how you spend your money is a concrete step towards making changes.

STEP FIVE: STOP BEING AN OSTRICH

This is when I want you to pull your head out of the sand and stop being an ostrich. How do I know that's what you're doing? Well, anyone who is not comfortable, clear about and happy with the way she or he handles money is being an ostrich about money in some way.

Being an ostrich means being in denial - in other words, hiding, pretending or ignoring a truth about the way you spend your money. As long as you do this, you will never feel in control of money or really good about the money you have. It's the same as tying a blindfold around your head, then wondering why you're always in the dark when it comes to your financial situation.

What are the ways in which you're being an ostrich? Be honest with yourself. Are you doing any of the following?:

☐ Ignoring bank statements or bills.

☐ Running up credit-card debts.

☐ Keeping a permanent and dangerously swelling overdraft.

☐ Depending too much on something you can't afford at the cost of areas where you should be putting your money.

☐ Trying to keep up with people who have more money than you.

☐ Trusting that everything will somehow work out in the end.

☐ Getting caught in the grip of a spending obsession - shoes, bags, clothes.

☐ Comfort spending to avoid painful feelings.

☐ Attempting to buy love.

☐ Pretending to be someone you're not in order to impress.

☐ Gambling excessively in any way.

☐ Submitting to blackmail.

☐ Supporting another adult who is capable of supporting himself or herself.

☐ Investing in something suspect or uncertain.

☐ Promising yourself a fresh start with money - over and over again.

If you're doing any one of these things - or several of them - you're being an ostrich. Time to stop! Why? Because being an ostrich is:

* Uncomfortable.

* Difficult and stressful to keep up.

* A waste of energy and time.

* A way to keep yourself poor.

* A manner of inviting things to get worse.

* Always unrewarding and often damaging.

When you decide to stop being an ostrich, you'll feel a surge of relief and you'll be taking a big step towards financial freedom and abundance. All you have to do right now is to become absolutely clear about where and how you're being an ostrich. Once you've recognized what you're doing, you can choose to stop. Have you had enough of burying your head in the sand, of the uncomfortable feelings that go with it and of living in a financial fog? Great! Then make the decision to stop. Today.

Leave being an ostrich in the past and know your worth.

STEP SIX: TAKE CONTROL

Today I want you to make the decision to take control of your money and the way you use it. Most people, if asked to think about it, feel that money is controlling them and not the other way around. Even the phrases people use give this attitude away. Do you ever use, or hear, the following?:

"I wish I could, but I haven't got enough money."

"If only we had the money."

"I hate money."

"I never have the money for what I really want."

"Money's such a bore."

"Money just disappears."

"I don't know what happens to it all."

"I dread bills - they just eat my money."

"The cost of things these days is horrific - I can't afford the things I want."

It's as though the money chose to disappear, or chose the way it was being spent, rather than you managing it. Make an effort today to watch the way you talk about money and to stop using phrases that make you sound weak and powerless in relation to it. Instead, begin to think of yourself as strong and successful with money. Recognize that the way you spend your money is your choice.

Instead of saying: "I can't afford it", say: "I'd rather save my money for other things."

Instead of "I hate money", say: "I love money, it brings all kinds of good things into my life and I enjoy managing it well."

Instead of "Money just disappears", say: "I always know how much money I have and what I'm choosing to spend it on."

Instead of "I dread bills", say: "I pay my bills with pleasure, knowing I can afford them and appreciating the benefits and services they bring."

Instead of "The cost of things is horrific", say: "I always choose to spend my money on things which are good value and worthwhile."

Changing the way you talk and think about money will revolutionize your attitude towards money and bring more of it into your life. Begin to think, talk and behave as though you are in clear and firm control of your money, and refuse ever to think of things the other way around. Instead of letting money be an overlord, a burden or a source of worry, choose to make it an ally, a source of freedom and a pleasure.

Choose to say no to resentment, frustration and lack. Say yes to control, to calm and free choice, and to plenty.

Be in control of your money and know that the choice is yours.

STEP SEVEN: WHAT YOU WANT

This is the step where you're going to have fun making your financial wishlist. Before you start listing all the things you'd love to buy and have and do, however, I want you to think very carefully. Don't rush straight to the statement bag, the skiing holiday and the expensive beauty treatments.

On this wishlist, I want you to put the things which would really bring you peace of mind, a sense of security and joy. They may not be the things you think of first. Sometimes, the biggest benefits come from spending your money on things which seem boring and worthy. It may surprise you, when you think long and hard about it, to find out what you really want.

Here are some ideas for your wishlist:

* Buying your own home.

* Paying off your mortgage if you already have one.

* Accumulating savings.

* Joining a pension fund (the younger you start, the cheaper they are!).

* Learning about wise investments.

* Having enough ready for Christmas so that you don't end up flat-broke in January.

* Knowing that you have enough and are comfortable.

* Never borrowing money again.

* Never fearing bank managers/landlords/credit-card companies again.

MY WISHLIST

It's easy to wish for sudden wealth and to imagine that this would end all your problems. The reality is, however, that most people are very unsettled by sudden wealth. It takes them out of their comfort zone and catapults them into a whole new set of challenges and problems.

It's better by far to be wise enough to know what would work well for you and what is sufficient. How much would you need in order to feel comfortable and happy? To stop worrying? It's probably far less than you imagined at first, as the real art of comfort and freedom from worry is good management and abundance consciousness.

By all means include fun things and luxuries on your wishlist. In fact, they're very important - everyone needs them. But before you get to them, work out the basics, the things you need to put in place to feel great about your money and your life. Once you've identified these, think about a timescale for making them happen. Add this to your list, beside each item. So it might read: "Own my own home within three years, pay off debts within six months, start saving now."

Know that everything on your wishlist is possible, and that it's up to you to make it happen. Think about the steps you'll need to take to begin doing this. Feel the joy and pleasure of knowing that it's up to you and that you can grant your own wishes.

<u>Wish for what you want and make it come true.</u>

STEP EIGHT: KEEP IT SIMPLE

It's time now to begin managing your money in ways that you can sustain for the rest of your life. The wonderful thing about managing money is that, once you've got the hang of it, you never forget it again - just like riding a bicycle or salsa dancing!

The best truth of all is that managing money is simple and should always be kept simple. If anyone tries to make it complicated or tells you it's complicated, don't believe them. It isn't, and it need never be.

To manage your money well, you need to observe some basic rules:

* You must know what you spend.

* You must know what your income is.

* Your spending must be less than your income.

* You must keep an accurate, up-to-date record of all your income and spending.

And that's about it.

What you don't need are endless accounts books, 15 bank accounts, complex computer spreadsheets and daily study of the financial newspapers. Here's what you need to organize your money in a simple and effective way:

* A current (checking) account with a bank, building society or credit union.

* All your regular bills paid automatically from your current or working account.

* A savings account.

* A regular payment from your current or working account into your savings account, so that your savings grow almost without you noticing.

* One credit card which you use for emergencies only - or at the very least judiciously - and the bill for which you repay in full each month.

* Online access to your balance, which you check daily.

* Online access to past bank statements and other financial documents.

* A couple of hours once a month to check your bank statements against your records and to pay any outstanding or one-off bills.

These can all be organized if you put your mind to it. So set the wheels in motion - today. Once your money management has been simplified, your whole life becomes simpler. You'll free up time and energy for other things, and money worries will diminish.

Remember that it's always best to know what you have - and what you don't. That way, you can make decisions about what needs changing and about what you spend. Avoiding knowing simply causes problems. To know what you're dealing with is to choose solutions over worry and wisdom over ignorance.

Keep it simple and choose to be a winner with money.

STEP NINE: WHAT GOES OUT

Take the next step in managing your money well. In order to put the first of the basic rules in place, you must know exactly what you spend. If you haven't organized and managed your money before, this will probably be a grey area. It may be a bit blurry round the edges or it may be a complete fog! Whichever it is, don't worry. Just make the decision to dispel the mists and to come clean with yourself about what you spend your money on.

Use the list on the next page, adding any other categories that apply to you. Now begin to fill them in. You need to know what you spend on a monthly basis. Use any documents you have that will help, such as bank statements, bills or receipts. Where you don't know the amount, put an estimate. When you've finished, you'll have an idea of what you spend. It's unlikely to be completely accurate, but it will give you something to work from.

Over the next month, write down in a notebook every single amount you spend, however small. Carry the book around with you and get into the habit of noting any money you spend as soon as you spend it. You won't need to keep doing this for ever (unless you want to), but it's important to do it for at least a month, or even two or three, so that you know exactly what you are spending. You may find that some of your estimates were way out. You may be surprised by how much you spend on food, cosmetics or fuel.

If you live with a partner or friends, you must work out your share of the expenses. It's vital that things are fairly divided and that you agree on this. You can then take care of your share and let the other person or people deal with their side of things.

Writing down all your spending is an eye-opening exercise and one that is well worth doing. You'll never again be able to say: "I don't know where it goes!" You'll open the door to choices and flexibility in the way you use your money.

Know what goes out and you have the key to change.

WHERE DOES YOUR MONEY GO?

Rent or mortgage.   ....

Bills - gas, electricity, phone.   ....

Insurance - house, car.   ....

Club/gym memberships.   ....

Credit-card bills.   ....

Store-card repayments, rental agreements.   ....

Food.   ....

Clothes and accessories.   ....

Cosmetics and toiletries.   ....

Entertainment and leisure.   ....

Travel (not including holidays).   ....

Car and car expenses, if you have one.   ....

....

....

....

....

....

STEP TEN: WHAT COMES IN

So, you have dealt with how your money goes out. Now you need to look at the money that comes in - in other words, your income, from whatever source. In order to manage your money in a simple and satisfying way, this half of the equation has to be filled in.

The previous exercise may have been tough. You may have been amazed by the amount you spend. This step should be more fun, even if you think your income is too low. As you do today's exercise, think abundance. Feel rich at the thought of the money that comes to you. Recognize how lucky you are and that this money is yours, to use as you choose.

WHERE DOES YOUR MONEY COME FROM?

Write down all the regular elements of your income, no matter how small the amount. Make sure you include (if applicable):

* Earnings from your job/s.

* Grants.

* Interest on savings.

* Dividends.

* Rent paid to you.

* State benefits.

* Maintenance for yourself or your children.

Add any other categories that apply to you. Now fill in all the categories, using wage slips; bank, building society or post office records; and any other relevant documents you have. At the end, add everything up to come up with a monthly income total.

Now you need to compare this figure with the monthly expenditure figure that you worked out yesterday. To achieve financial peace of mind, it's essential for the income figure to be higher than the expenditure figure.

If your income figure is higher than your expenditure figure, that's fine. You have a good basis from which to work. You can think about using any excess for saving, paying off any debts and loans, or having a "fun" fund. If the two figures are about even, that's okay, too, as long as you're happy with the way you're spending your money and don't mind not having a safety net. If the expenditure figure is higher than the income figure, you need to make changes.

Don't panic and start planning to move, live on baked beans or cancel your phone contract. Do, however, think about what would be needed to bring your figures into line. Perhaps you could earn more? Perhaps you could make fairly simple adjustments, such as buying fewer clothes? Perhaps you need to make bigger changes, such as moving somewhere cheaper or selling your car. It's your decision, and it's you who will feel the benefits.

Know what is coming in and appreciate these riches.

STEP ELEVEN: BE HONEST

Today it's time to look at whether you're totally honest with yourself - and other people - about what you do with your money. Don't be alarmed by the idea that you might be less than truthful. Almost everyone is, often without even realizing it. It takes courage and integrity to venture into every dusty little corner of your finances and to be absolutely honest with yourself. But it's worth doing, as it will bring you peace of mind and freedom from worry.

Think about what might be going on that's less than completely honest. If you've got debts, that's a clue, as we often kid ourselves and fib to ourselves to justify debt. Here are some ways in which we're not always upfront about money. See whether any of these apply to you:

☐ You keep money secrets from the people to whom you're closest.

☐ You make excuses to yourself to justify credit-card debts or loans.

☐ You accept money gifts (for instance, hand-outs from your parents), even when they make you feel uncomfortable and childlike.

☐ You count the same bit of income three times when making spending decisions.

☐ You never look at bank statements and bills.

☐ You put things on credit cards when you know you can't afford them.

☐ You know you need to make changes, but you keep putting them off.

☐ You fiddle your tax.

☐ You tell lies about money to another person - anyone at all.

☐ You rely on your partner for an income when there's no good reason why you shouldn't earn your own.

There are many other ways in which we can be less than totally honest about money. None of them feels good. Being dishonest, even in small ways, leaves you feeling bad about yourself. Even if no one else knows you're cheating, YOU KNOW!

Make the decision today to be completely honest. Begin with yourself. Root out all the secrets, tricks and cons, and junk them. Decide what you're going to do differently, and take action. Then tell anyone else who needs to know.

For instance, if you've decided to stand on your own two feet and stop taking money from parents or a partner, sort out what the alternatives are, then tell the person or people concerned in a warm and mature way. Don't forget to thank them for their generosity and support, even if you suspect that they may have used money to control you. Remember that it was your choice to accept it.

Or, if you never bother to check bank statements and bills, make a resolution to do so from now on. Schedule a regular time each month, and mark every one in your diary for the year. When it comes time to do it, look on it not as a chore, but as a challenge - a project you want to complete to the best of your ability and from which you can only gain. When you've finished, reward yourself with a treat. And, you never know, you may spot a mistake that means the bank owes you money!

Be honest, be clear and set yourself free.

34

STEP TWELVE: THE COST OF YOUR JOB

It's time to look at the true cost of your job. This may sound strange at first, but it's important to understand that we all pay a price for the jobs we do and to be sure that you consider the price of yours worth paying.

What do I mean by the price we pay? Here are some examples:

* Working long hours.

* Being undermined or put down by someone.

* Becoming a monster who orders everyone around.

* Doing something too easy for you and feeling frustrated.

* Having to make all the decisions and feeling alone and unsupported.

* Being a part of something which doesn't fit with your beliefs.

* Doing something which damages your personal life.

There are many other potential downsides to any job. It's very important that you recognize any that affect you and weigh them against the good aspects of your work. Of course, the good aspects may far outweigh the price you are paying. If so, that's fine. But be true to yourself. Never hang on in a job through fear that you won't find another one or won't succeed elsewhere. There is always another possibility, always an alternative, always the potential for a fresh start.

People who love their work tend to be the ones who succeed financially too. Doing something you love will motivate you to give your best, and it may bring you rewards such as promotion, bonuses or a pay rise. But there are also people who hang on in jobs they hate because the money is good. If you are one of them, think again. Money alone is never a good enough reason to compromise your wellbeing. If you work for money alone, you'll never truly enjoy the job and feel good about it. Feel proud of the way you earn your living and you'll be able to enjoy your money and attract more of it to you.

Spend today weighing up the price you are paying for your job. If you feel, deep down, that it's time to make a change, begin to look around for a job which is truly right for you. Expect to be fairly rewarded, but don't be driven by money. If you take care of yourself by finding the right kind of job for you, the financial side will take care of itself. Be brave, be bold and be proud of what you do.

If the price you pay for your job is too high, find the courage to let it go.

STEP THIRTEEN: CANCEL THE CRISES

This step is devoted to money crises and what can be done about them. Are you one of those people who has regular money crises? Is your financial life a constant rollercoaster of highs and lows that create all sorts of problems? Are you often in the middle of some kind of financial drama or upset? If so, it's time to look at different ways of doing things.

Here are some examples of financial crises. See whether any of them apply to you:

☐ A huge bill has arrived, and you can't pay it.

☐ Someone you borrowed money from wants it back right now.

☐ The money from the remortgage/loan you took out has all gone and you need to borrow more.

☐ The credit-card company is threatening to take you to court.

☐ The mortgage/rent is in arrears.

☐ The money you're expecting hasn't arrived and your bank account is empty.

☐ You've gone over your overdraft limit yet again, and you're being stung for massive interest charges.

- [ ] The hot-water system has blown up and you can't afford a new one.

- [ ] Payday is two weeks away and you're broke.

- [ ] The gas/electricity/Wi-Fi has been cut off because you didn't pay the bill, but you don't even remember receiving it.

- [ ] You've had to grovel to the bank manager/your parents/ your landlord yet again, and you're getting sick of their patronizing expressions.

Does any of this seem familiar? People who go in for financial crises tend to have them regularly and to experience a variety. They're tedious, scary, exhausting - and exasperating for everyone else. So why does anyone do it? It's partly lack of good money management, but there's another part to it. Every financial crisis has its pay-off - in other words, its reward. Often this is the relief when the crisis has been sorted out. People who lurch from one crisis to another are often addicted to the feelings of anxiety followed by relief. But the good news is . . .

You need never have another financial crisis again!

It's that simple. Make the decision today to reorganize your finances, to live within your means and to put money aside for emergencies. Free yourself from the burden of financial crises. Get off the high-low rollercoaster, and give yourself the gift of peace of mind. Use the skill with which you sort out crises to avoid them in the first place.

Financial crises drain you - let them go and feel the freedom.

STEP FOURTEEN: SHARED FINANCES

This step is for focusing on the question of shared finances. It may be that you already share some financial responsibilities with another person. Perhaps you have a flatmate or a partner. If you don't, you can be sure that you will, at some point, need to make joint financial decisions with another person and to share your finances with them.

Between friends and flatmates, these issues should be easily sorted out, as your money stays separate. You simply decide who is responsible for what. If complications arise, you can deal with them or move on. Between partners, however, financial issues are more complex and can become a source of conflict. So, it's just as well to get the rules really clear from the start, so that you're prepared for the best way to manage things and need never let money come between you.

Everyone has a different attitude towards money and different ideas about what's important. Finding a way to agree on the basics and live with the differences is one of life's most valuable skills.

MANAGING JOINT FINANCES

1 Always keep your independence. Have a joint account for joint responsibilities, but keep your own account, too, containing some money which is yours to spend as you wish.

2 Never hand over the management of finances to the other person. It's fine for one of you to do the day-to-day accounting, but the other one should know what's going on and join in all decisions. If you leave everything to your partner, you put yourself in a childlike position; if you're the one who does it all, you may end up feeling burdened and over-controlling. Either way, you'll both be resentful.

3 Decide which areas of expenditure are joint, and either allocate them between you or both pay money into a joint account to cover them.

4 Be honest with each other about what matters to you. If you want to save but your partner wants to spend, work out a compromise and stick to it. Always listen to the other person's point of view, and be willing to negotiate. Let go of the idea that one of you is right and the other is wrong.

5 If you stop work - for instance, to have children - make sure that you still have spending money of your own. You're still contributing to the family, and you shouldn't have to ask your partner for every little bit of money you need.

6 Plan for a future that isn't completely dependent on staying together. Divorced women often end up poor because they relied too much on their husband's earnings. Have your own assets and money that will be yours no matter what.

Organizing your finances jointly is a challenge for most couples, especially if you've managed your money on your own for a long time. Do it gently, with humour and understanding. Even if you come up against a frustrating and difficult situation, remember that miracles can be worked with tenderness and love, whereas anger and criticism will only create blocks.

Learning to manage money with another person can be exciting, fun and rewarding.

STEP FIFTEEN: MONEY MISTAKES

Okay, this is the point where you have to face up to money mistakes. Why? Because every single one of us has made them and will make more of them. No one manages money perfectly, and most people get quite a lot of things wrong.

Perhaps you've even made the same mistake twice - or several times. If this is the case, there's something important to be learnt from this type of mistake, and, when you learn it, you will no longer need to keep making it. Life often gives us the same lesson over and over again until we learn what we need to know.

So, if you're feeling bad about any mistakes you may have made, large or small, relax. Mistakes are simply there to show us the way forwards and to teach us how to manage better in the future. Learn from them, and they become gifts.

Here are some of the mistakes that people commonly make. Do any of them strike a chord with you?

☐ Splashing out on something which turns out to be a dud, such as a timeshare holiday apartment you hardly, if ever, use or an expensive outfit you never actually wear.

☐ Spending more than you earn and having to borrow to make up the difference.

☐ Investing in something which goes bust or loses value badly.

☐ Thinking that spending money will magically make you feel better if you're feeling low or broken-hearted.

☐ Taking on financial responsibilities that you think you can cope with, then finding that they're just too expensive and you're constantly worrying.

☐ Lending money that you never get back.

If you've made any of these mistakes, or any others that aren't listed, you should take comfort from that fact that you're not alone. These mistakes are all very common. The good news is that you need never make them again.

AVOIDING MONEY MISTAKES

* Think very carefully before you spend any large sum of money. It's easy to be drawn into the excitement of a phone upgrade or a new outfit, or anything else. But it will generally always be there the next day (despite what they say!), so consider it overnight, check it out thoroughly if necessary and only go ahead if you're sure.

* Impulse buy with only very small amounts of money.

* If you want to go out and spend to cheer yourself up, decide how much you can afford to blow and only take that amount with you in cash.

* When you take on the responsibilities of a mortgage, work out what you think you could afford, then reduce it by a third. It's better to have money to spare than to be trapped with costs you can't manage.

* Never lend money that you can't afford to lose. Either treat the loan as a gift or refuse to make it.

* If in doubt about any purchase, resist the temptation.

Of course, everyone makes mistakes, and you are bound to continue to make a few in the future. Follow these guidelines, however, and they'll only ever be small ones that you can easily sort out.

Look on every mistake you've made as a step towards good money management.

STEP SIXTEEN: DEALING WITH DEBT

Today it's time to look at debt. Most people have debts of one kind or another. The essential thing is that you feel you can manage any debts you have and that they're worth having. If not, it's time to start getting rid of them and to think about the thrill of being debt-free - and, if you've ever worried yourself sick about debt, you'll appreciate that being debt-free genuinely is a thrill!

When you take on any debt, you must decide whether it's worth the price to you. A mortgage is a debt, and most people feel it's worth taking it on to have a home they will eventually own. Almost all debts, however, cost a lot in interest. Before you buy anything on a credit card or a repayment deal, work out the interest you will pay and the REAL cost of the item. A dress can end up costing twice as much as the price on the tag if you pay for it in monthly instalments on a credit card. A car can cost you half as much again than the cash price if you pay for it over three years of financing. Only you can decide whether it's worth this kind of cost to you. Remember, if in doubt, say no.

A DEBT ACTION PLAN

Perhaps you already have debts that you're worried about. Here's what to do:

1 Look at the interest you are paying on each debt. If it's high, or if the monthly repayments for all of them add up to more than you can afford, ask your bank or building society to give you a loan that will allow you to repay all the debts. You can then pay off the loan, which should be at a more reasonable rate of interest, over a longer period and at lower monthly instalments.

2 If you really feel in crisis over debt, go to a debt-counselling agency for advice. There are plenty of them around, and their experts will help you to sort it out and deal with creditors.

3 Steer clear of loan agencies offering you instant loans - they usually entail very high interest charges.

4 Remember that being in debt doesn't make you a bad person. It simply means that you aren't managing your money well. Make the decision today that you will deal responsibly with your debts, then begin to manage your money well.

Debt is a drain on you and your money. The simple truth is that life is better without debts. They can cause anxiety, stress, sickness and premature ageing. Deciding to live without debt (apart from a mortgage, which is acceptable debt) is a decision for freedom and a burden-free financial life.

What's the downside of saying no to debt? It may mean going without something you'd like to have, saving up for what you want or making do with an old model. Is that really so hard? Only if you let it be.

Debt is a burden you can live without - leave it behind.

STEP SEVENTEEN: ABOUT THAT RAINY DAY

I want you to think about savings. Do you save? Or do you think that it's something you'll get around to when you're richer/older/better organized? Well, here's a useful tip:

Nothing makes you feel richer than saving your money.

Almost everyone dreams about winning big or earning an immense sum of money. They fantasize about the wonderful feeling it would bring, about all the things they'd do with the money and about never having to worry again. For some people, the dream does come true. Even if you do win, earn or inherit a fortune, however, you won't feel rich for long if you spend it all. Hanging on to some of your money is the key to feeling rich. And that's a fabulous feeling.

Also, the fact is that only a handful of people achieve sudden riches. So, while it's fine to dream, do it at the same time as using the money that you do have in the best possible way.

THINK YOU CAN'T AFFORD TO SAVE?

Think again about not being able to afford to save. You can begin with just a small amount, but do it regularly, every month. Make an automatic payment into a savings account. Once you've organized it, forget about it. Don't be tempted to raid your savings - let them mount up and, when you can, increase the amount you pay in. Every time you remember that you have money saved, you'll feel good about it and so feel good about yourself.

Don't rely on dreams alone. And don't kid yourself that you'll get round to saving when things are easier. Saving will help to make them easier because it turns your thinking around. If you can afford to save, you must be doing okay and managing your money well. The more you believe this is true, the more you'll continue to manage better and better.

Make the decision today to keep more of your money. Money is for spending, but it's for spending wisely, not rashly. What could you do without in order to put a little money into your savings? Do you really need that new pair of gadget/outfit/meal out? Or would you rather keep your money? There is always a choice, and, if you usually choose to spend, it might be fun to make a different choice and see how it feels.

Don't be tempted, though, to oversave. Hanging on to money too tightly is never a good thing. If you never spend and try to hoard it all, you stop the flow of money in and out, and you may find less money coming to you. Always remember that life is about finding balance, and so is good money management.

Begin saving today and feel richer every day.

STEP EIGHTEEN: ATTRACTING MORE

Prepare to feel excited. This day is all about how to attract more money into your life and how to feel rich and fill your life with plenty. The wonderful thing is that, once you tune into abundance on one level, say, money, you'll find it easy to attract abundance in other areas of your life, such as love, success and happiness.

First of all, there's nothing wrong with having plenty. In fact, there's everything right with it. Having plenty doesn't mean that you're greedy, selfish or depriving others. The main thing stopping you from having plenty may well be your beliefs. If you believe that you don't deserve money, or that you must stay poor or that you will always let money slip through your fingers, this is precisely what will happen.

Decide today that you will choose to believe in abundance and to attract wealth of every kind into your life.

ATTRACTING ABUNDANCE INTO YOUR LIFE

1 Always focus on abundance beliefs, such as "I deserve to have plenty", "I attract money easily", "I always have more than enough". Repeat these positive phrases to yourself if you find yourself worrying about money.

2 Start to notice the riches that come into your life. Notice when other people are generous to you, when you find a coin in the street, when you get a lower bill than you expected or a small win or a rebate of some kind. All these things are abundance coming into your life. When you notice them and appreciate them, you will attract more of them, and greater amounts.

3 Be clear about what you want. Rather than saying: "I want to be rich," decide what exactly it is that you want right now. For

instance, you may want enough money to buy a car, or put down a deposit on a house or apartment.

4 Be generous. The meaner you are, the less you will find good things coming into your life. Generosity always attracts more to you. But don't give simply in order to get. Learn to give lovingly, without expecting anything in return. Give to charity, give little gifts to family and friends, give time and energy. This doesn't mean spending recklessly, but give what you can and never let fear of poverty stop you giving.

5 Think lucky. Imagine you are the luckiest person you know. Imagine everyone you know saying to you: "How on earth do you do it, you just seem to get lucky all the time?" Walk around with a big smile on your face, feeling lucky. It won't take long for it to come true.

6 Cultivate an attitude of gratitude. That is, be thankful for all that you already have - your job if you have one, your possessions, the holidays and treats that come your way, the things you are given. Be grateful for your talents and abilities, your family and your home. Every night, instead of asking for more or thinking about what you don't have, give thanks for what you do have.

Follow this today and every day for the rest of your life. Make it part of who you are. Become known for being generous, relaxed with money and a lucky person. Expect to attract abundance into your life and you will.

In order to attract more, you need to believe that more is coming.

STEP NINETEEN: BE YOUR OWN BEST ADVISER

I want you to make the decision today that you are your own best money adviser and that you won't allow anyone to make you feel stupid when it comes to money. There are plenty of people around, including professionals such as accountants, bank managers and financial advisers, who are keen to put you down and make you feel ignorant in an effort to sell you their products. Some of them do this in a very friendly way, so that it's easy to be taken in.

Of course, there are times when we all need to consult experts, and there are experts who will treat you like an intelligent person and give you wise advice. And that's the point. It's up to you to know the difference and to choose whom you consult about money matters.

A GUIDE TO USING THE EXPERTS

* Never, ever hand over all the decision-making about your finances to someone else, whoever they are.

* Trust your instincts. If something doesn't feel right, don't go ahead with it.

* Check everything out. If you're told that a particular product is the best, check it out yourself. Do some research to find out whether that's really true.

* Never make an instant decision, particularly if you're being urged to do so. Always think about it for a day or more, and consider the alternatives.

* Make absolutely sure that you understand what you're being offered or advised to do, and what the long-term consequences may be.

* Don't be afraid to ask experts to explain something in simple, clear terms. If they can't or won't, they're either no good at their job or trying to sell you something you should avoid.

* Bear in mind that only you know what you want and what will suit you best. That's why you are your own best adviser. No one else has your interests at heart in the same way.

Understanding financial matters does not have to be complicated or mysterious. If you want to open a savings account and you're not sure which is the best kind for you, shop around and compare interest rates and the terms and conditions. For instance, an account with a good interest rate may not allow you instant access to your money. Think about what you need and what will suit you.

Refuse to be a dunce. Never say things such as "I'm no good with figures" or "I just can't understand financial things." Always tell yourself: "I am great with figures, I can understand anything I need to." Train yourself by taking leaflets and information home and reading them carefully, without pressure. Remember that you can take the time you need to understand what you want to understand.

Decide today to be wise and clever with money and to trust yourself.

STEP TWENTY: STAY INDEPENDENT

In this step I want you to assess how independent you are when it comes to money. To be financially successful and to manage your money well, it's important to be independent. That is, you need to make your own decisions, to take charge of your own money and to generate your own income, unless there is a particular reason why you can't.

Many otherwise competent adults remain childlike in relation to money, depending on others or reluctant to take charge of their own finances. Are you among them? If so, it will hold you back and limit your options.

Depending on others is the same as giving them power over you and putting yourself in a weak position. If you're doing this, today is the day to reclaim your power and shout it from the rooftops.

Here are some of the ways in which people commonly keep themselves from being financially independent. Do you do any of these?

☐ Relying on hand-outs from parents.

☐ Accepting an unearned income from a partner, or anyone else, when there is no good reason why they shouldn't earn their own income (obviously the situation is different if they're bringing up children, studying, ill or caring for a relative).

☐ Borrowing from friends or family.

☐ Relying on someone else to make financial decisions for them.

☐ Having no bank or building society account and relying on someone else to process cheques.

☐ Blaming someone else for their financial problems.

....

....

....

....

....

....

....

If you recognize any of these, or if you've noted down other ways in which you keep yourself from being financially independent, it's time to make changes. Financial independence is great for your self-esteem, it's exciting and it's enabling - you'll have far more freedom of choice when you stop relying on others.

Whatever excuses you're using to stay dependent on others, be willing to give them up. Many adults still rely on their parents, believing that this is okay because their parents hand over money willingly. But once you're an adult, you shouldn't need money from your parents (or anyone else who's bailing you out). Stand on your own two feet, and feel good about yourself.

Here's what to do to be truly financially independent:

* Earn your own income. Give up excuses such as "I can't find the right job", "I hate working" or "I just want to do one more training/study course."

* Never borrow money without a clear, written agreement stating when you'll pay it back - and always stick to it. It's better to borrow from a bank than a friend, as this means it is clearly a business agreement.

* Open your own bank account and manage it yourself.

* Make your own financial decisions. Of course, it's fine to ask advice from people you trust, but make sure that the ultimate decision is yours.

* Stop blaming others. Take responsibility for the outcome of your financial decisions, even the mistakes.

Financial independence is precious and worth having. Decide today what you need to do to be truly independent. Thank anyone who's been helping you, then let go of the life rafts, take the plunge and swim on your own!

Be financially independent and welcome success into your life.

STEP TWENTY-ONE: MAKE GOOD CHOICES

Now that you're making your own financial choices, it's crucial to make sure that they're good ones. You need to know that you are wise and clever enough to make choices that will bring you stability, security, prosperity and peace of mind. You don't need to be trained as an expert or to have unique skills to make such choices. All you need are simple guidelines and confidence in yourself.

GUIDELINES FOR MAKING WISE CHOICES

1 Find money mentors. By this, I mean people whose judgement and skill with money you admire. They needn't be experts. You may well have a friend who is good with money and who always seems well organized and competent financially. Ask him or her to teach you what they know.

2 Acquire the skills you need. If you think it would be useful to learn how to use your computer's accounting software, or to improve your maths ability, go ahead and find a relevant course that would suit you.

3 Always apply the simplicity rule: when looking at any financial choice, assess whether it's simple enough for the average person to understand clearly. If it isn't, don't go for it. Cons and bad deals are often wrapped up in complex jargon so that people won't spot them.

4 Decide whether something is right for you. We're all individuals with different needs and different life plans. That's why only you can know whether a financial decision is right for you. The way you organize your spending must be built around the lifestyle you want.

5 Calculate whether you can afford it. This is really the key question. Never be tempted to overstretch financially. Nothing's more miserable than struggling to keep up with payments and demands. Always allow a margin, or comfort zone, and plan on things costing more than you expect.

6 Never rush any financial decision. Take time to think about whether it's right for you. So many mistakes are made through haste, and shysters and salespeople know this all too well. People selling anything from timeshares to washing machines will try to draw you in on the spot, insisting that the deal is only available right now. Never fall for this one - a good deal doesn't need to be rushed.

One of the key elements of making good decisions is knowing that there is always a choice and that the position you are in now is the result of choices you've already made. If they haven't been so great, decide today to turn things around and begin making good choices. You'll find that things improve very fast once you do.

Never make a choice in order to please other people. If they don't like the choice you've made, then that's okay. If they're disappointed or angry, remember that this will pass and it's not your responsibility. Your responsibility is to do the right thing for you, while respecting and not hurting others. If you give in under pressure, it will damage your self-esteem and your relationship with the other person.

Take your time and make the right choices for you.

STEP TWENTY-TWO: MONEY FOR FUN

Feel free to remember that money is not just for serious things; it's for having fun with as well. Being too frugal, duty-bound and solemn about money will only make you miserable - not to mention everyone around you. No matter how tight things are, it's still important to put a little money aside just for fun and play.

Money is not meant to make you feel guilty, miserable or burdened. It is there to make your life good, and, the more wisely you spend it, the more you'll enjoy life. Having fun is part of wise spending. After all, what's the point of working hard, planning well and organizing your money if you forget to enjoy the fruits of your labour?

WHAT IS FUN TO YOU?

Grab your pen and write down ten things you really enjoy. They might include riding a rollercoaster, visiting a comedy club, skiing or swimming, dancing the night away, enjoying a midnight picnic or going on a shopping spree. Or you might love spending a day on the beach, indulging in beauty treatments or meeting friends in a café.

Of course, not all ways of having fun involve spending money. But some do. Once you know how you want to have fun, you can build it into your spending plan. If you're part of a couple, you might decide to plan for things you can do together, such as a special meal out, a weekend away or a trip to the theatre.

There's another aspect to fun and money, and that's to learn to take troubles more lightly and to use your fun side as a resource. The most important time to have fun is often when you feel least like doing it - when things are difficult, when there seem to be problems all around you, when you feel broke. Sometimes the breakthrough comes when you can approach your problems in a humorous and light-hearted way. Or it comes after you have let yourself forget your problems and simply enjoyed yourself. You can then see things in a whole new light.

Remember that nothing is so awful that you can't laugh about it. Try saying your problem out loud, then add "Ha, ha!" at the end. For instance, "I've no idea how to pay off my debts. Ha, ha!" It may sound crazy, but your problems will seem less awful and less daunting, I promise. Being able to bring a light touch to a serious situation is a great skill to have. Laughter can help untangle knotty situations when nothing else can. I'm not suggesting that you be irresponsible. Only that you use the power of humour, fun and lightness to help you solve problems.

People who know how to have fun are special. Although we seem to possess this ability naturally as children, most of us lose it as adults. If you find that you tend to be too serious and never have fun, take a fresh look at your life. You may decide it's time to make some changes.

Do something fun today. Laugh, play and enjoy yourself. Let yourself be happy, and let money help you have fun.

You deserve to have fun and enjoy yourself with your money.

STEP TWENTY-THREE: GOING WILD

Look at those times when you decide to go wild, to splash out and to say: "To hell with it, I'm going to spend no matter what." Almost everyone has moments like these. Christmas is a prime example. For many people, despite promising themselves to cut back or to be careful, a sudden rush of spending fever overwhelms them and they shoot way over budget or stick things on credit cards, caught up in a wave of excitement and promising themselves to deal with it later.

Bank managers know this syndrome well. So do all financial advisers. Christmas is the most tempting time of all, as mass spending is going on. If everyone else is doing it, why not you, too? It's a bit like mass hysteria - very, very catching.

Why not join in? Here's why not:

* Picking up the pieces after overspending is demoralizing and exhausting.

* After the wave of excitement comes the wave of worry - it lasts a LOT longer.

* Two months after Christmas, almost everyone will have forgotten what you gave them. In one recent survey, not a single schoolchild asked could remember, eight weeks on, what their parents had given them for Christmas.

* The items which seemed so essential, so exciting and so worthwhile at Christmas will often be gathering dust in a cupboard a few months later.

* If you pay for something with a credit card, then pay off that amount in monthly instalments, the final cost of the item will be three to four times the original price. With this in mind, look at potential purchases and quadruple their price before you buy. Are they still so exciting?

If you want to go wild at Christmas, plan it! Work out, roughly, what you think you spent last Christmas. That's how much you need to save before this Christmas. The best way is to divide the amount by 12 and set that sum aside each month. When Christmas comes, you just spend what you've saved. Forget credit cards.

Other "go wild" times such as birthdays are just the same. By all means enjoy them, celebrate and be generous. But don't spend for the sake of it, and don't spend money you don't have. You can always choose to make presents instead; there are loads of things that anyone can make very cheaply. Or set a limit for each present and look on it as a challenge to find something lovely for under that limit.

The truth is that going wild just isn't worth it if it takes you into financial hell. The grovelling to bank managers, scrimping and scraping afterwards cancel out the brief thrill of the overspend.

Count the cost of going wild before you do it.

STEP TWENTY-FOUR: COMFORT SPENDING

Look at those times when you decide to go wild, to splash out. Most of us comfort spend from time to time, and that's fine. Some people do it so much, however, that it tips them into financial hardship, and this is when the problems really start to multiply. Instead of bringing comfort, their spending simply causes more misery, which in turn often leads to more comfort spending, creating a vicious circle.

Comfort spending is what you're doing when you spend money to make yourself feel better. The idea is to take the focus off unhappy feelings, whether they be loneliness, anxiety, depression, a broken heart, grief or any other painful feeling. Spending money on something you like gives you a temporary buzz, a lift, which masks the unhappy feelings. But the buzz is brief, and it's often followed by a low. So you need to spend again to get the buzz back.

This is what is happening with shopaholics. Usually women, shopaholics spend and spend, getting into debt and amassing cupboards full of things they often don't ever use or even unwrap. The point about this kind of comfort spending, just like any addictive behaviour, is that it doesn't work. In the long run, it won't help at all with the unhappy feelings - in fact, it only intensifies them.

Do you have any comfort-spending habits? Do you reach for a credit card when you feel low? Buy another round of drinks? Spend money you don't really have or could use more wisely on something else? If you do, it's time to stop. This is not as hard as you might think. Once you understand why you comfort spend, you can choose to change the pattern.

GUIDELINES FOR CONTROLLING COMFORT SPENDING

1 Don't be afraid of painful feelings, whatever they are. Try saying to yourself: "They're only feelings. If I'm miserable, that's okay, there's nothing terrible about it and nothing I have to do to fix myself." Painful feelings fade much sooner if they're acknowledged and not suppressed.

2 If you want to comfort spend, set yourself a spending limit which won't damage your bank account. Take that amount with you in cash and don't spend any more. Cut up your credit cards if you are often tempted to use them for a quick fix.

3 Give yourself some real comfort. Comfort means feeling safe, warm, comfortable and cosy. Try curling up with a soft blanket, a scented candle and a good book. Find out what really gives you comfort, then do it when you feel down. Perhaps it's a walk in the woods, a chat with a friend or a hug from someone who loves you.

Make the decision today to stop damaging comfort spending and to give yourself real comfort when you need it. Comfort means being kind to yourself, not creating problems for yourself.

Swap comfort spending for true comfort and feel the difference.

STEP TWENTY-FIVE: GIVE IT AWAY

Today I'm going to encourage you to give your money away. Yes, I do mean it! Few things in life are more satisfying, uplifting and rewarding than being generous to others. It has the added bonus of drawing money to you and increasing your abundance as well.

When money is tight, people are in debt or they're having trouble managing financially, they tend to go one of two ways. Either they're overgenerous, giving away money and presents which they simply can't afford to buy, or they become mean, hanging onto every penny and only grudgingly buying gifts when they have to. Does either of these patterns sound familiar? To which group do you belong?

If you're overgenerous, it may be what got you into financial difficulties in the first place. Being overgenerous is the result of wanting approval and to be liked - which means your self-esteem is low. Being mean stems from poverty-consciousness, fearing there isn't enough to go round and that you have to hang onto what you've got. In both cases, people confuse money with love. Overgenerous people think they can buy love. Mean people think they won't be loved, so they must hang on to the crumbs they have and look after themselves.

If your behaviour with money follows either of these patterns, take today to stop and think about what you're doing and decide to change the pattern. Swap what you're doing for true generosity. Cultivate this in yourself - you will feel better about yourself, better about life and better about money.

True generosity means giving:

* Because you really want to, just for the sheer joy of it.

* Without expecting anything in return.

* What you can afford.

* With love, from your heart.

* When the time feels right, not because the calendar says you must.

Bear in mind, too, that the other side of giving is receiving. In order to give generously, you must be able to receive and accept generosity from others. Most people find it is far easier to give than to receive. Do you put obstacles in the way of receiving from others? Are you grumpy and ungrateful, or embarrassed by or feel uncomfortable with acts of generosity towards you? If so, you can begin to turn these feelings around. Being unwilling to receive means you feel you don't deserve good things and acts of love. Tell yourself today: "I deserve all the love and generosity which comes my way. I will receive it with joy."

Don't forget that both giving and receiving begin with you. Give yourself small gifts and acts of kindness. Receive them willingly and with pleasure. By both giving and accepting abundance, good fortune and acts of kindness with an open heart, you will attract more of them into your life.

To give and to receive are both acts of love.

STEP TWENTY-SIX: LOOK AFTER THE SMALL CHANGE

It's time to ponder the little things in life. Why? Because it's the things you spend small amounts on which you justify to yourself most easily and which all too soon add up to large amounts indeed.

Think about the time you take to make a decision about a really big purchase, such as a house, a car or even a holiday. You want to know exactly what's involved and whether it's a good investment. With small outlays, it's often very different. You fancy that miracle new face cream, gorgeous bracelet or cute handbag, and snap it up without thinking for more than a nanosecond or two. You probably justify it to yourself, telling yourself that you can afford it, you'll live cheaply next week, do without something else. The truth is, however, that for most of us this happens over and over again. And these "small" things become big!

Lucy was a teacher living in a large city and sharing an apartment with a girl with whom she wasn't getting on. She was fed up because she never seemed to have any money and couldn't afford a place of her own. On top of that, her old car was about to fall to pieces, and she couldn't afford a new one.

After a month of life coaching, Lucy had turned her life around. She took a long, hard look at her finances and realized that she was spending a lot of money on extras she didn't really need. Top of the list she compiled were shoes. She would buy a new pair every week and had cupboards full of them. Lucy made the decision to stop throwing her money away and start saving. Six months on, she had bought a car in good condition and put a deposit on an apartment of her own.

Analyze your spending to see how many "small" things you purchase and where you could save. What have you got six of that you don't even use? Could you take lunch to work instead of buying it? Could you buy cosmetics more cheaply? Borrow a dress instead of buying one? Give a friend a gift you made yourself instead of buying one? Walk to work sometimes instead of taking the train or bus? Give up convenience foods?

The point here is not that you have to live like a pauper or do anything you hate doing. It's that when you take a long, hard look at your spending, there is often so much money which goes on little things you barely notice and which end up simply taking up space or being thrown away half-used. Once you realize this, you can choose where to cut back and keep your money, and where you want to spend it.

Do it today!

EXERCISE

Write down your last three impulse buys, then think about how important they are to you now. The thing you just "had to have" has probably already lost its allure, hasn't it?

....

....

....

Now identify three areas where you can cut back your spending, without causing yourself any hardship. Write down the amount you will save daily, and see how much you will have saved after a month. That's money you still have and can choose to save or to spend on something else.

....

....

....

When you think carefully about smaller buys and choose to skip some of them, you suddenly find that you have more money than you thought possible. It's liberating!

Feel instantly
richer by choosing
to say no to the
non-essentials.

STEP TWENTY-SEVEN: MONEY AND MOODS

It's time to reflect on the link between money and moods. We all have moods - they're simply a part of life. And moods change, like the weather. When your mood is good, your spirits are high and things feel easy. When your mood is bad, your spirits are low and worry and anxiety can easily set in.

Your mood can have a significant impact on the way you handle money. When you are feeling low, everything seems harder, other people seem better off, making or managing money feels like hard work and success looks a million miles away. In a low mood, problems seem overwhelming. In a great mood, the very same problem can appear small, manageable and unimportant.

THINK ABOUT A RECENT WORRY YOU'VE HAD

Perhaps you were anxious about a bill, an overdraft or a fall in income. You probably focused on it a lot, turning it over in your mind many times. Now imagine you have just had the most amazing piece of good fortune. Perhaps you fell in love. The feeling of being in love is wonderful; the world glows with joy. In this light, your problem looks small. You know you can handle it. You make a decision about what to do easily, without fretting.

This is the effect that moods can and do have. It's important to recognize when your mood is clouding your judgement and when you should put off financial decisions. Never try to solve problems or waste time worrying about them when you feel low. You'll just make yourself feel more depressed and solve nothing. Self-pity is like treacle: you get stuck in it and, the more you struggle, the deeper you go.

The next time you feel a bit blue, make a decision to put off all worry and anxiety about money. Tell yourself: "I'll deal with that later." Wait for the mood to pass. You can speed this up, if you want to, by talking to yourself in positive ways and being kind to yourself. When you're feeling good again, you can give some time to sorting out your finances and making decisions.

Remember, too, that problems, like wounds, often heal themselves if left alone. Picking away at a scab makes it worse. So does worrying about a problem over and over again. Leaving it alone and trusting that all will be resolved often leads to a solution, sometimes without you having to do a thing.

Be patient with a low mood - it will pass, often much sooner than you expect. Be glad of a good mood and enjoy it. And always be aware of the effect your mood is having on the way you handle your life and your money.

Make money decisions when your mood is good and make things easy for yourself.

STEP TWENTY-EIGHT: TRUST

Today I want you to look at the issue of trust in relation to your money. Do you trust yourself to handle money well? Do you trust others with whom you have to share financial matters? Do you trust that you will always have enough and need not worry? For most people, the answer is yes in some areas and no in others. For some, there is no trust anywhere. Yet trust is vital if you are to feel relaxed and successful when it comes to money.

What or who don't you trust around your money? To trust is to have faith that the outcome will be for the best or that people will do what they say they will. Trusting yourself is the same. It means having faith in yourself to cope and to do what you set out to do. It's about believing that all will be as it should be.

Begin with your instincts. Trust yourself to know who will treat you and your money fairly. Stop dealing with anyone who won't. Look at the behaviour of others. Is it straightforward, honest and reliable? Above all else, look at your behaviour in relation to money. Has it been less than trustworthy in the past? Have you promised yourself to do something but not done it? If so, you can begin to turn this tendency around. There are bound to be other areas in your life in which you have been totally trustworthy. Knowing this will show you that you are capable of being trustworthy. Now believe that you can handle money in the same way.

LEARN TO TRUST YOURSELF

Make three agreements with yourself today. Put them in writing and stick to them. They might include agreeing to:

* Pay your bills within three days of receiving them.

* Update your accounts once a month.

* Pay back any money you owe within a certain time.

* Stop spending on certain items.

* Keep within your budget.

* Buy yourself a small treat once a week.

* Sort out your tax/pension/will.

* Save a small amount every month.

Keep to these agreements you have made with yourself, and you will soon begin to trust yourself. An agreement with yourself may not seem important - after all, you can break it, and no one else will know that you have broken it. But it's actually more important than any other kind of agreement. Keeping an agreement you have made with yourself gives you a sense of being authentic, honest, trustworthy and worthwhile. It boosts your self-esteem and will give you more of a buzz than any spending spree can.

Keep trust with yourself and know that you are worth a million.

STEP TWENTY-NINE: SET YOUR AIMS

Dedicate this step to working out your aims for the future and deciding what your goals will be in your financial life now that you have examined it more closely. So far you've done a great deal to get your finances in order and to take charge of your money and manage it well. By now, you will be feeling more confident, more in control and more optimistic about money than you ever have before. This means it is the perfect time to look ahead and decide where you want to go from here. Doing this will give you goals to work towards, keep you on track and reinforce the new habits you have learnt. It's all too easy to let things slip and find yourself back in a mess again. Choose not to do this, and decide instead to keep money matters simple and effective.

EXERCISE

Write down the money goals you have for the future. Here are some of the things you might want to include:

* Being completely debt-free.

* Managing your money without needing credit cards.

* Saving regularly and building up a really significant amount.

* Owning your own home outright.

* Earning money doing a job that you love.

* Reviewing your finances once a month.

* Being more choosy about how you spend your money.

* Learning all you need to know about financial matters relevant to you so that you can continue to be your best adviser.

Add any other financial goals you'd like to achieve. Now divide your list into long-term aims (such as owning your own home, changing your job) and short-term ones (keeping up your spending record, becoming better informed). Think about what's going to be involved in keeping on track and reaching your goals. Do you need to open an extra savings account to build up a deposit to buy an apartment or house? Do you need to start looking for a job that you enjoy more and which also pays more? Do you need to boost your positive beliefs about yourself and money by repeating them to yourself out loud each day?

Goals are great, but you won't achieve them unless you take action, consistently, to work towards them. This takes willpower. Old habits will still feel easier than new ones for a while. Decide now what your money habits are going to be, and stick to them until they're automatic and you've forgotten your old habits completely.

Knowing what you want is the key to success. Most people have only a vague idea of what they want and what it will take to get it. Be different: know what you want and bring it into your life with positive beliefs and action.

Aim high and know that it's up to you to make your goals a reality.

STEP THIRTY: CELEBRATE!

Well done! You made it through to the end. If you have carried out the challenges set for you, you will have given your finances, and your attitude to money, a complete overhaul. I hope that by now you're not afraid to handle money, you're aware of just how talented you are with money and of the great potential for success that you have, and you trust yourself to be your own wisest financial adviser.

I hope, too, that you now know how to attract abundance into your life. I trust that more and more is coming your way every day and that you're enjoying every minute of it. I know that you will be making wise choices and that often your choice will be not to spend, but to keep your money and enjoy the sense of security and plenty - not to mention self-control - that this brings.

Here are the things I want you to celebrate about you and your money:

* You can attract what you need, and what you want, into your life.

* You have power over your money and won't hand control to anyone else.

* You can afford to be generous and can enjoy receiving, too.

* You know who to trust and who not to trust with your money.

* You will never allow any "expert" to make you feel small or ignorant.

* You truly value what you have.

* You know how to comfort yourself without spending money.

* You are independent and make wise choices when it comes your money.

* You know the secrets of good, simple money management.

* You know how to have fun with money.

So much to celebrate! If you have these skills now, you can carry them with you for the rest of your life and never be afraid around money again. Remind yourself that, even if disaster hit and you lost your job or all your possessions tomorrow, you would cope. You would pick yourself up and carry on, as what you can never lose are the inner resources that lead to success.

Be proud of yourself, and enjoy your money. After all, that's what it's for!

Celebrate the joy
of being successful
with money - now and
for ever.

A FINAL WORD

You're now firmly on the fast track to the financial success that you deserve. Nothing can stop you from being successful with money if you really want to be and believe that you can be.

While financially things have been tough all around the world in recent times, it's important to remember that money is energy and as with all energy sources, there are universal laws which govern it. Energy needs to keep moving, not to remain static. This is why it's important to keep money flowing in and out smoothly, and to be generous. With money energy, like attracts like. Hence the more you have, the more you will attract. As with other energy sources, there is plenty of money in the world, enough for everyone. Poverty is the result of our misuse of this valuable resource.

You absolutely can choose to make money your ally, your support and a great source of pleasure. Just like having a fit and toned body, having a fit and toned financial set-up makes you feel great. You have all the resources you need to stay in charge of your money for ever and to create the financial life you both want and deserve. So go for it!

CAREER

Every single one of us deserves a career that is exciting, fulfilling and rewarding. A career that uses our talents and abilities, one which makes going to work something to look forward to and challenges us to reach greater heights of achievement. If you're not in a career that you love and feel enthusiastic about, it's either because you haven't yet found what it is that you want to do or because you have still to learn how to best tap into the deep well of courage and motivation inside you which will propel you towards what you want.

We are all capable of far more than we imagine. We each have hopes that we long to realize. It is largely our doubts and fears that stop us from pursuing them. Whatever you want to do with your working life is probably not only possible, but also right for you. We may need to adapt them slightly along the way, but our dreams are always in keeping with who we are.

So, whatever you're doing now, whether you're working, not working or studying, the time has come for change. That's why you've picked up this book. You are ready to move on from the boredom, frustration, unhappiness or confusion of your current situation.

Follow these steps and by the end you will see your working life in a whole new light. You'll be aware of your strengths, filled with healthy confidence, able to make the right choices and speeding along the path towards the career of your dreams.

"I NEVER DREAMT OF SUCCESS. I WORKED FOR IT."

ESTÉE LAUDER

STEP ONE: CAREER AND YOU

Work. Who wants it? Who wouldn't rather spend their days lounging around, spending money on designer clothes or meeting friends for lunch and catching up on the latest gossip. Work is a pain, a necessary evil, something to get through in order to get paid. Right?

Wrong.

In fact, if you think like this you'd be wrong on every count. As surveys have found, those who are "lucky" enough not to have to work are often miserable and have problem-filled lives, drug and alcohol dependencies and messy relationships. The ones who survive best find a project, such as a charity, to immerse themselves in, to give them a purpose in life.

And that's the point. We may all, from time to time, wish that we didn't have to work, but having to work is really a blessing. Why? Because work is the greatest source of self-esteem and fulfilment that we can ever have. If you want to feel good about yourself, do a good job. It's as simple as that.

What isn't always simple is finding the right job for you. And that's vital, as the wrong job, or even the right job in the wrong place with the wrong people, can make you very, very unhappy.

From the day we start until the day we retire, work takes up an average of around 50 years of our lives. That means we work for about 11 years of our lives. And often it's more, as many of us put in longer hours, begin when still very young or work past the usual retirement age.

Finding the right career means the difference between spending those 11 years feeling miserable and spending them feeling happy. It means discovering your talent, your potential and your ability. It means testing yourself, going for what you want and feeling the buzz that comes when you have a real sense of achievement.

Whether you have found it yet or not, there is a right career for everyone. Some people find it easily, some even know what it is almost from the day they can walk. Others need to wait, to explore, to venture down a few wrong alleys before they reach it. If you are one of these, don't worry - now is the time to find out exactly what it is you want to do and to go for it. And if you already have an idea of what you want to do, but think it's beyond you, the next 30 days will show you just how wrong you are. It's probably much closer than you imagine.

So, today, on your first step of working towards the career for you, I want you to promise yourself that you won't stop until you find the career that's really right for you. You deserve nothing less.

The perfect career is waiting for you right now.

STEP TWO: WHEN YOU KNOW IT'S WRONG

Something is wrong in your working life. Otherwise you wouldn't be reading this section of the book. You would be out there conquering the world in your chosen career.

Consider whether any of the following statements are true of you:

Do you identify with any of these? Tick the ones that apply:

☐ I'm hopeless with money.

☐ I'll never earn much.

☐ Other people have plenty of money, not me.

☐ Money just slips through my fingers.

☐ I don't deserve to have money.

☐ Money is dirty - you can't be rich and be a good person.

☐ I'll never be in control of my money.

☐ Bills and demands are scary - I dread them.

☐ There isn't enough money to go round.

☐ I'm always afraid that my money will run out.

If any or all of these are true of you, it's time to stop vaguely hoping that things will improve of their own accord or telling yourself that you have to stay in this job.

Now that you have identified the symptoms of your unhappiness, you need to look at the causes. Here are some examples of what you may be experiencing now. Think about whether any of them ring true:

☐ Your job is boring and unfulfilling.

☐ Your boss is unkind and puts you down.

☐ You work with difficult people or with one person in particular who makes your working life hell.

☐ You believe your job or the company is morally wrong because it hurts people or animals in some way.

☐ You trained for something, but now you're not sure you really want to do it.

☐ You were pushed into your career by parents or teachers, and have found that you simply hate it.

☐ You know you could do a whole lot better than your present job.

☐ You want to earn more.

☐ You know what you'd like to do, but you haven't the confidence to go for it.

☐ You work ridiculous hours.

Perhaps there are several things here that apply to you, or you may have other reasons why you're not in the right job. You may not have a job at all, and your quest is to find one. Whatever the case, don't despair!

The first step to getting it right is to know when it's wrong.

STEP THREE: TIME FOR CHANGE

Admitting that something is wrong in your working life and that you deserve better may well bring with it a feeling of relief, even if there's some fear and uncertainty, too. Perhaps you've been telling yourself that you can handle it, that you're lucky to have a job at all, that it will all work out, that you'll grow to like it better or that the person you can't stand will leave.

Sometimes these things do turn out to be true. But it's rare. It's better to decide that you will be the one to leave or make changes. Why stay unhappy in the hope that things will improve when you can make them better for yourself now? This way, you take the power for change into your own hands, instead of waiting for someone or something else to change.

Think about how you talk about your work to family and friends. Do you find yourself saying any of the following?:

☐ It's a job - what else can I say?

☐ It'll do.

☐ It's okay, I suppose.

☐ Today wasn't so bad.

☐ I hate it.

☐ When I think that I've got to work for another 35 years, I can't bear it.

☐ Oh well, who does like their job?

☐ It wouldn't be so bad if the money were better.

☐ I can't believe some people get to do something they like and be paid for it.

☐ I love it when I have the flu - it means I have a genuine reason to miss work.

If any of these resonate with you, you need to make changes. No one should have to put up with a work situation that isn't right, whatever the reason. Sometimes we can put up with a temporary problem, such as long hours, if it moves us towards a goal worth having and if we know the downside won't last. Unless this is clearly the case, however, problems at work need solving. The solution is either to make changes in your present job or to leave and find another that's right for you. This does take courage and self-confidence, but the very first step is simply to say:

"I won't put up with this any longer."

Say this to yourself, loud and clear, and *mean* it. Say it with confidence, even if you don't yet have any. Once you decide to make changes, big or small, you are giving yourself permission to get out of a situation that is wrong for you.

Once you've decided to make the changes, you will find that there's no going back. The part of you that is determined, excited and ready for change will take the lead, even if there's another part which is much more scared and unsure!

Making changes is
a way of giving
yourself gifts.

STEP FOUR: WHY ARE YOU THERE?

Today it's time to ask yourself an important question: why are you doing the work you're doing now? Something led you there and something has kept you there so far. You need to ask yourself this, as in any situation there are benefits. It's human nature that we never stay of our own free will in a situation that is all bad. There's always a pay-off for us, even in something that at first seems pretty grim.

When you identify what the pay-off is, it will help you to see what you want next, what might make it hard for you to leave and how it is that you chose this job and stayed for this long.

What is your pay-off? Write down the following:

The pay-off for me in choosing this job was . . .

....

....

The pay-off for me in staying so far has been . . .

....

....

Think about the reason or reasons you stay in a job which does not make you truly happy - there will be one at least, even if you're not consciously aware of it. Here are some ideas that may help, if you can't immediately detect what the pay-off is:

You chose the job because:

☐ The money was good.

☐ It seemed to promise security.

☐ You thought it would be easier to find other jobs if you were in a job already.

☐ You thought it had potential.

☐ It was the first job that came along.

☐ It was a job of which your parents approved.

You've stayed so far because:

☐ You like the people.

☐ No one makes too many demands on you.

☐ The money's good.

☐ You're scared that any other job would be worse.

☐ The job fits in well with your social life.

☐ Your family or partner thinks you should stay.

Think whether any of these ring true for you and come up with more reasons of your own. No job is all bad; there's always an explanation for why you chose it and why you stay. Now that you have an idea of what that is, you can use the information to help you decide on your next move.

For instance, suppose you've stayed because you have friends at work and a nice working atmosphere. This tells you how important it is to you to get on with the people with whom you work. This requirement should therefore be high on your list of priorities for your new job.

Or suppose you like the money and you think no other job will pay you as well. There's nothing wrong with enjoying the money, but the idea that you can't earn it doing something else is false. It's always possible to be well paid while doing something you love. You can have the money and add on job satisfaction and challenge as well.

What about pressure from parents, family or a partner? This tells you that their opinion is important to you. So you'll need to explain carefully to them why this job is wrong for you and that you need to make changes. Ask them for their support and encouragement.

STEP FIVE: MOVING ON

Okay, now it's time to get yourself unstuck and to rev up your motivation to find the career that's really right for you. You know that your job isn't right for you and that you want to do something that is exciting, challenging and rewarding, and which makes going to work a joy. You know why you've stayed so far and what matters to you in a job. That's progress. Now I want you to think about the reasons for being in the right job and the right career for you, no matter what it takes to get there.

WHAT ARE YOUR BELIEFS?

Write down things you believe about you and work. These might be:

* There's no such thing as a fun job.

* No one would pay me to do something I actually enjoy doing.

* Life would be great if only I didn't have to work.

* I don't really have any special skills or talents.

* Work is what you have to do to make possible the fun parts of life.

* Everyone hates work, don't they?

* People like me just don't have great jobs.

* I'd never have the courage to go for a top job.

* People would laugh if I told them what I really want to do.

* The only point of work is to earn a living.

....

....

....

....

....

....

....

....

....

....

....

....

....

....

Pick the ones which sound true, then come up with your own. Underline the two or three that feel most important. These are the beliefs that hold you back, keep you stuck and crush your self-belief and motivation.

Now search for any positive beliefs you have about you and work. For instance:

* I always do any job very well.

* I feel satisfied when I've done a good job.

* People in my family have always had interesting jobs.

* I know there are things at which I really excel.

* I could go to the top in the right job.

Take any of these that are true, add your own beliefs, then produce some new ones. For instance:

* I have the talent and ability to do anything I want to do.

* Work is one of the best things in life.

* I deserve a career I really love.

* I deserve to be well paid.

* I deserve to be appreciated at work.

* I can have fun and get paid for having it.

....

....

....

....

Add more positive beliefs as you think of them. Now make the decision to throw out any negative beliefs you have about work and to stick instead to your new list of positive ones. Write them down and put the list up where you'll see them often. Carry another copy around with you and repeat them to yourself whenever you can. Gradually, you'll learn these beliefs by heart and they'll become true. Look around you for examples of other people who already have these beliefs and who are in jobs they love, being well paid and appreciated.

When you have these kinds of positive beliefs, your motivation and self-belief are high, you're raring to go and you know the right job is just around the corner.

Believe you can have the perfect job and you will.

STEP SIX: WHAT IS SUCCESS TO YOU?

It's time to think about what you really mean when you talk or think about success. Everyone would like to be successful, but success means something different to each one of us. Truly successful people live according to their idea of success, not other people's. Trying to succeed in the eyes of others often leaves us frustrated and unhappy.

There are plenty of examples of people in careers in the world of finance who make huge amounts of money but aren't happy and who then switch to something more low-key and feel much more fulfilled. One man gave up his lucrative, 14-hour-a-day insurance job to be a builder and to spend more time with his wife and young children. Many people thought he was mad, but he was wise enough to know what would make him happy and that this would feel like true success.

EXERCISE

Write down: My idea of success is . . .

You might include any of the following:

* Plenty of money.

* A gorgeous home.

* A job I find exciting.

* Recognition from others.

* Being creative.

* A powerful job which influences others.

* Dressing in designer clothes.

* Feeling that my skills are in demand.

Add any other ideas that you have. Keep this list and refer back to it later. Remember that you can add or take away anything at any time, as your ideas change and your career progresses.

Society's idea of success is certainly linked to money and power. These things can be fun and exciting - if they're what you want. The most important criterion for success, however, is personal fulfilment. That means feeling challenged by what you do. It means always wanting to be the best you can be and having to find the very best in yourself in order to do your job as well as you possibly can.

Working in a job which brings no challenge and demands very little of you will soon become boring and frustrating. Knowing that those you work with will expect the best you can give and will set you challenges which stretch, excite and motivate you, by contrast, makes it far more likely that you will love your job. And loving your job is the best sign of success that there is.

Each one of us is entitled to career success, and it is absolutely possible for you - and everyone around you - to do what you really want to do and to be successful in your chosen field.

Know what success is to you and go for it.

STEP SEVEN: THE RIGHT JOB FOR YOU

So what is it that you really want to do? What job is going to lift your spirits, make you want to leap out of bed each morning, reward you with a good income and give you a sense of achievement and fulfilment? What is it that will allow you to use your talents and abilities, work in an environment you like and plan the future you want?

For each one of us, there are at least two different careers that we could follow very successfully. Most of us have several more than that. Don't think that there's only one career for you and that you must find it and only it to achieve your potential. Instead, bear in mind that there may be a few careers you'd love, that you have a number of options and that it's up to you to choose what you'd like to go for. Once you've chosen, it is still possible to change your mind, at some stage, and try a second or even a third career. Many people make a big success of two or three quite different careers. Like the city stockbroker who became an osteopath. Or the computer whizz who went on to make stained-glass windows.

Finding out what's right for you involves two steps. The first is identifying what it is you'd love to do. The second is believing you can do it. Today, you're going to begin taking the first step - towards finding out what it is that you really want to do.

EXERCISE

Write down all the things you love doing. Don't try to relate them to work at this stage - just put down anything that comes into your head and which you love doing. Your list may include cooking, walking in the woods, talking to people, writing a journal, swimming, eating out or travelling.

....

....

....

....

Now look at the list you've made and see what patterns begin to emerge. How might some of the things you love doing fit together?

Begin a list of jobs which would include at least two of the things you love doing. For instance, suppose you love cooking, meeting people and organizing events. All these qualities would be needed to open your own restaurant. Or suppose you love to spend time alone, to be in the open air and to paint. Becoming a garden designer would be one of your options. On the other hand, you might love being around lots of people, feeling the buzz of working at a fast pace and working with mathematics. Add city dealer to your list.

Be as creative as you can about this list, so that you end up with at least five jobs which would incorporate some of the things you love doing.

> When you know what you love doing, you'll be well on the path to the right job for you.

STEP EIGHT: YOUR TALENTS

Today, I want you to look at all your talents and skills, so that you can add even more options to the list of potential careers you could have. Before you ask: "What talents and skills?" - stop. Everyone has them and most of us have far more than we ever imagine. There are things you do every day, without even thinking about it, which entail all kinds of skills, talents and abilities.

EXERCISE

Write a list of your ten top skills and talents.

You might include:

* Good organizational skills.

* Punctuality.

* An excellent memory.

* Being good with adults or children, or both.

* A reassuring and calming manner.

* Being funny and entertaining.

* Sound writing skills.

* Musical ability.

* A mathematical bent.

* Being a reliable and sensible driver.

....
....
....
....
....
....
....
....
....

Now write a list of ten useful things you've learnt through experience. You might include:

* Being organized works better than being in chaos.

* You know how to manage someone who has drunk too much at a party.

* You prefer small groups of people to large ones.

* You have learnt how to let the angry behaviour of others bounce off you.

* Standing in front of an audience gives you a buzz.

* You can rise to a challenge.

* You're the best judge of what's right for you.

* You get back as much as you put in.

* Life is full of surprises.

* Sometimes you get exactly what you want.

....

....

....

....

....

....

....

....

....

....

....

Add to both of these lists, and begin to build up a picture of just how skilled and talented you are and how much you already know about life and work.

Now write a third list. This time note ten things you'd bring to any job. For instance:

* Enthusiasm.

* Organizational skills.

* Staying power.

* Energy.

* Quick thinking.

* Ability to learn new things.

* Ability to get on with others.

* Care and thoughtfulness when carrying out tasks.

* Ability to look ahead and see possible problems.

* Willingness to tackle difficult assignments.

By now, you will be able to see that you have a great deal to offer in whichever career you choose. And that's a wonderful feeling.

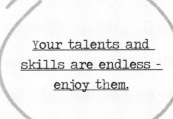

Your talents and skills are endless - enjoy them.

STEP NINE: YOUR PLACE IN THE TEAM

Now it's time to think about how you like working with other people. This is vitally important for your future career, as the more you know about how you like to work in a team, or even whether you do like to work in a team, the easier it will be to find the right working environment for you.

The wisest people know what makes them comfortable in relation to others at work. Some people love to lead, to make the decisions and be in charge. Others actually hate the pressure of this role and work much better when directed by others or in parallel with others. Some people prefer to work alone as much as possible. So which are you? Answer these questions to find out.

ARE YOU A LEADER?

- ☐ Do you love to be in charge?
- ☐ Do you enjoy decision-making?
- ☐ Do you often see what needs doing when others are confused?
- ☐ Do you get frustrated when you're overruled?
- ☐ Do you see other people's strengths?
- ☐ Are you a clear and quick thinker?
- ☐ Do you often have new ideas?

DO YOU PREFER WORKING ALONE?

- ☐ Do you find that noise, chat and interruptions ruin your concentration?
- ☐ Do you feel happy in your own company?
- ☐ Do you hate the idea of having to work jointly with others?
- ☐ Do you hate office restrictions - the hours, the travel, etc?
- ☐ Do you find that you are more creative and get a lot done when you're working alone?
- ☐ Do you find it easy to start work and to keep motivated?
- ☐ Do you work well without feedback from others?

Tick the questions that you answer with a yes, then see how many ticks you have in each section. The one with the most positive answers is likely to be your preferred way of working. If you have the same number of yes answers in two sections, you may not know clearly yet how you like to work. This will emerge over time and will give you valuable direction for the future.

Everyone needs to work in the best possible way for them. Too much or too little responsibility for others can be frustrating and undermining.

You'll work best when your place in the team is right for you.

STEP TEN: YOUR IDEAL WORKING DAY

Today you're going to have fun creating a picture of your ideal working day. Imagine you could have the perfect working day. What would it be like? This is a day during which you feel fulfilled, challenged and energized. A day when you get up feeling great and go to bed feeling even better, having enjoyed every minute.

It's entirely possible to have a working day like this, but to ensure it you have to know what it looks like for you. Some people's ideal day might be in a busy office in the middle of town. Others might prefer a quiet studio beside the sea. You don't have to think about the specific job you're doing - this is about your working environment, the hours, the people and your pace.

EXERCISE

Write down an outline of your ideal working day. Include the following details:

When did you arrive?
Did you begin work at 6 am, 10 am, lunchtime or in the evening? We all have a particular time of day when we feel at our best, and this could be a great time to start your working day.

Where are you?
Are you in a big office full of people; alone in a cool, beautiful studio; or in a jazzy little business with just a handful of people?

How did you get here?
Did you stroll over from home, five minutes away, sit on the top of a bus, cycle, drive or travel by train?

What are you doing?
Are you at a desk, constantly on your feet, being quietly creative, walking around while you think out solutions or dealing with a dozen different demands at once?

With whom are you working?
Are you with a fun bunch of energetic, talkative people or with a boss you really respect and from whom you learn? Are you organizing others or simply working quietly alone?

What is it about this work that feels good?
Is it the buzz of pulling off a deal, the joy of being creative, the positive feedback you're getting, the challenge to come up with solutions?

Who is paying you?
Is it one person, a corporation, a charity?

How much are you being paid?
Loads of money? Just the right amount - which isn't loads, but does nicely? Not much, but you don't care?

Why are you being paid instead of somebody else?
What is it about you that makes you right for this job? What are those special qualities which mean that you are the one chosen to do the work?

This exercise will give you
additional information about the
way in which you'd like to work.
You can add this information to
all the other information you've
collected about yourself so far,
and see what kind of picture is
emerging. Now you're getting much,
much closer to finding out what it
is that you really want to do.

You can have your
ideal working
environment every day.

STEP ELEVEN: THE SECRET DREAM

I want you to look deep inside yourself and find your secret dream. Every single one of us has a dream - something we long to do, something which inspires us and which we like to imagine ourselves doing. In most cases, however, we dismiss it as impossible. "Why should I be so lucky?" we ask ourselves. "How could I hope to do something like that?"

Sometimes your dream is already there in your life, but simply not as your job. It might be something you do in your spare time, something you have a flair for and really look forward to doing, but for which you never imagine being paid. In other cases, the dream is buried so deeply that there's no sign of it at all. You might be living a life that is totally different from your dream and wondering why you feel unfulfilled and that your working life is "not right".

Here are some examples of people who made their dreams reality:

Cat was a very successful fashion model, but she was miserable. Throughout her life, people had told her she must use her beauty and laughed at the idea of her doing anything else. But she knew she wanted something else. Eventually, Cat found the courage to leave modelling behind, train as a counsellor and start helping people - what she'd always secretly wanted to do.

Jo was doing well as a human resources manager in a big company. But she found her job boring and couldn't wait to rush home every evening to work on her house, decorating and designing it room by room. She had already moved five times and each time she had decorated the house and created a stunning home. Jo never imagined she could be paid for doing what she really loved. She decided to give it a try, however, and she's now a very successful freelance interior decorator.

Paul worked for a big accountancy firm and, although he was successful, he felt depressed when he thought about staying in the same kind of work for the next 30 years. His secret dream was to write a novel. He worked on it in his spare time and didn't tell a soul because he thought people would laugh. But it was Paul who was laughing when his novel sold for a lot of money and he became a full-time writer.

Stories such as these happen all the time. You can keep your secret dream a secret and carry on with something that isn't right for you. Or you can bring out the dream, polish it and nurture it, making it come true.

Remember:

* No one has a secret dream that is wrong for them. What you dream about is the best clue to what you should be doing and will be good at. Living your dream as closely as possible is the way to be true to yourself.

* To live your dream takes courage. Beware of people who tell you it's impossible; they may say this because they haven't made their own dreams come true.

* If you don't know what your dream is, write lists of the things you love doing and the things you long to do. See what jumps out at you. Or look around at what others are doing and see what excites you.

* Making a dream come true will take hard work, determination and sticking power. Don't let any hurdles stand in your way.

<u>Your secret dream will show you which career is right for you.</u>

STEP TWELVE: YES I CAN!

Still feel that your dream is a world away from what you're doing now?
Do you think that perhaps other people can make dreams come true, but
it seems impossible for you? That your life is just too full to leave any
space for chasing dreams? If so, it's time to put the Yes I Can! plan into
action.

To make a dream come true, it is not enough just to know what that dream
is. You have to believe in yourself, your talent and your potential. And
that's what Yes I Can! is all about. It helps you to lay the foundations
for the life you're going to lead - a life in which you have the career
you want and you are doing your job well, you are well rewarded and
feel valued by others. Before anyone else will value you, you must learn
to value yourself.

THE YES I CAN! FIVE-STEP PLAN

1 Name your dream
In other words, be proud of your dream and visualize yourself
making it come true. Write about it in a journal, paint it - do
whatever you have to do to make it feel more real. See yourself
as the person who has achieved the dream and feels fantastic
about it.

2 Encourage yourself
Look at the way you talk to yourself about your dream. Do
you criticize yourself, laugh at yourself, put yourself down?
Then stop right now. You're battering your self-esteem by doing
this. Instead, begin to talk to yourself encouragingly and
supportively. Tell yourself: "This is right for me, I can see
myself doing it, I'm ready to go for it, I have all the talent I
need to do this." Keep saying these things to yourself even if
they don't yet feel true. You'll believe them in the end.

3 Throw out limiting beliefs

Look for any limiting and negative beliefs you have about your dream and get rid of them! Start by writing them down. For instance: "I could never do that, people like me just don't make dreams come true, I'm much too boring/ordinary/untalented." Once you've written them down, burn the piece of paper. Now write out new, exciting beliefs you'd like to have and stick the list on a wall where you'll see them often. Whenever a negative belief pops up, just say no to it and begin thinking about a new, positive belief instead.

4 Get support

Talk about your dream with a few close friends whom you can trust to be supportive and encouraging. Don't tell everyone, as then you'll have to listen to people who discourage you, and that's just a waste of energy. If people don't believe in you, don't bother arguing. Simply smile and walk away or change the subject.

5 Like yourself

This is vital. If you don't like yourself, you'll never achieve your dream. Liking yourself means approving of yourself, appreciating your strengths and noticing all the great things about yourself which you never noticed before. See yourself as beautiful, full of energy and ideas, someone who goes for what she wants and gets it. Tell yourself, every day: "YES I CAN!" . . . And mean it.

Go through the steps of this plan today and every day from now on. Make it part of your life, part of the way you think and act. It will give you all the backing you need to make your dreams come true and find the perfect career for you.

You can do anything when you believe you can.

STEP THIRTEEN: YOUR DREAM CAREER

Today it's time to make the link between your secret dream and a real job that you can go out today to look for and which will lead you towards that dream.

Perhaps you think that your dream is totally unlikely and that you couldn't possibly earn money that way. Well, think again, as there's always a way to make the link between where you are now and where you want to be. No one has dreams which are wholly impossible. If your dream feels achievable, feels right, stays with you no matter what and means a lot to you, it's something which you can follow.

Imagine your dream is to skipper a yacht around the world, but you were seasick the last time you went on a short ferry ride. Imagine your dream is to be a top chef and run a restaurant, yet you can't even boil an egg. Imagine your dream is to be a pilot, but you can't even drive a car yet. Imagine your dream is to write novels, but you only scraped through English at school. Imagine you'd like to be a fitness instructor, but right now you get tired walking over to turn off the television.

Impossible? Absolutely not. Everyone who does something brilliantly couldn't do it before they started.

J. K. Rowling's first *Harry Potter* script was rejected by all major publishers before it was picked up by Bloomsbury. The most celebrated chefs couldn't cook before they learnt how. Every pilot has to start somewhere. Every fitness instructor worked up from zero to being as fit as they are today.

The point is not what you've done so far, but what you're going to do now. If you want to succeed, you must be clear about what you want, then start making it happen.

The would-be chef must get a job in a restaurant, even if it's only washing up. The would-be pilot must start acquiring the basic qualifications, even if this means going to night school. The would-be novelist must read and read and read and write and write and write. The would-be fitness instructor must begin going to classes and look at training schemes.

There's always a way, always a route and always a world of possibilities. Some of the people doing exciting, successful jobs today would have been written off as no-hopers early in their lives, but they were determined and refused to be put off. Plant yourself in their category: be one of those people who make their dream come true and do what you truly want to do. Amaze the people around you, prove the doubters wrong and give yourself one of the best gifts you can have - a career you love.

Do what you love doing and do your best.

STEP FOURTEEN: CREATE A PLAN

This is the day on which you are going to create a plan. To get from where you are now to where you want to be, you need a plan. This plan will be a career map, plotting your route to your dream career, with goals to achieve along the way.

Step 1

Write a description of what you'd like to be doing in five years' time. Imagine that by this time you are in your dream job. Of course, in reality you could be there sooner or it may take a little longer. That depends on what it is. But, for now, assume that in five years you're there: have fun visualizing your life and writing out a detailed account of the career you now have.

For instance, suppose you want to be a television presenter, with your own prime-time show to present.

Step 2

Now come back to the halfway mark, in two and a half years' time. What are you doing? How do you know that you are halfway to your dream job? What is your current job like, and are you enjoying it?

For instance, the would-be television presenter might be doing the links between programmes at this stage.

Step 3

Now imagine yourself one year from now. What are you doing that is taking you towards your dream job? Are you working in the same field? Is the work associated with the job you want? Are you having fun and do you know you're on your way?

For instance, the would-be television presenter might be working as a researcher or a production assistant for a television company, getting to know the right people and putting in applications for presenting jobs.

....

....

....

....

....

....

....

....

....

Step 4

It's three months from today. What are you doing towards your dream job? What decisions have you made? What changes and what moves have you undertaken?

For instance, the would-be television presenter might have started applying for all kinds of jobs in television, gone on a presenting-skills course and learnt a lot about how the television industry works.

Brilliant careers don't happen by magic. They are the result of research, hard work and effort. Often, the people who achieve them make them seem effortless. But they very seldom are. Most successful people have worked very hard. When you're working towards a dream, however, hard work doesn't feel so hard.

Most importantly, almost all successful people have had a plan of how to get where they wanted to be. In the United States, a group of university students were asked whether they had a plan for their future careers. Only 10 per cent had. Ten years later, that 10 per cent were all where they wanted to be. Almost all the others were not.

Create a plan and move steadily towards your dream job.

STEP FIFTEEN: GIVING IT SHAPE

Today you need to give your plan more detailed shape and direction. You've got the dream, you've made the plan and you can see yourself, in five years' time, doing exactly what you want to do, in the way that you want and the surroundings that you want.

Giving the plan shape is about filling in the details to get you to that end point. What exactly will be involved in getting there? Will you need to study, practise, raise money, get fitter, take courses or knock on doors until they open? Perhaps you'll need to go to someone at the top of your chosen career and ask advice or if you could assist him or her as a trainee. There are many routes and many things that will help you on your way.

EXERCISE

Start to add the details to your plan. Answer these questions:

1 What qualifications will I need?
Perhaps you have some qualifications already, or maybe you'll need to study to get some or to add to those you have.

2 Who can give me advice?
Is there anyone whom you trust who could help you plan your route? A good friend who understands what you want may have some great ideas to add.

3 Who can I learn from?
Who are the experts in your chosen career who might advise or teach you?

4 What training do I need to arrange?
Will you need to learn on the job as a trainee and/or to take a course?

5 What should I be practising?
In what areas should you be becoming an expert? Do you need to be fitter, to practise singing or playing an instrument, writing, cooking? Whatever skills you need, develop them as much as you possibly can.

6 What will it all cost?
This is important. If you will need to fund your training, you must think carefully about what the cost is going to be.

7 Where will the money come from?
Will you work while you train and earn your own way? Can you borrow some of it or arrange a training grant or loan?

Come up with as many answers as possible under each of these headings. Where you don't have the answers, make a note that you'll need to do research to find them. Fill in as much of your plan as you can, and keep adding to it over the days ahead.

Make sure that your plan includes what you want to achieve in one week, one month and every month after that for the first year, then every three months. As you achieve the first stages, you can fill in more detail on the later stages. Be ready to adapt your plan if you need to, but never lose sight of it.

Details give your plan the shape it needs to become reality.

STEP SIXTEEN: THE FIRST STEP

Well done! You've progressed halfway through this 30-step challenge, and you now know what your dream career is and have plotted your plan of campaign. So what comes next?

Today is D-Day, when you're going to take the first actual step towards making your dream a reality. All the plans and dreams in the world won't come to anything without action. So today is the day to get going and make things happen.

What is the first thing you need to do to set yourself moving on your path? Here are some possibilities:

* Look up information you need on the Internet.

* Call someone who can help or give information.

* Fill in an application for a job or course.

* Go to the place where you want to work and ask about jobs.

* Find out the name of a person at the top in your chosen career and email or call them, asking whether he or she can help you.

* Go to an exercise/cookery/photography/creative writing, etc., class.

* Go to a bookshop to find relevant books.

There are umpteen more possibilities. You just have to pick the ones likely to help you the most to do what you've chosen to do.

EXERCISE

Make a list of five things you could do TODAY to get started. Then do them. Start with the one you'd rather do last. It's probably the most useful one.

The easiest way to stop yourself getting started is to tell yourself you'll wait until you feel in the right mood. All too often, the right mood will never come along.

Feelings follow behaviour. This is a simple but invaluable truth. If you want to change the way you feel, change your behaviour. So, if you're sitting around waiting to be hit by a "get-going" feeling, forget it. Just get going and the feeling will follow. This is one of the biggest secrets of people who succeed. They do what they need to do regardless of how they feel or whether or not they want to do it.

Furthermore, they keep on doing it, and they don't let anything stop them. So, go on. Take that first step, then keep on, taking the next step and the next . . .

Take the first step, and walking 1,000 miles will seem possible.

STEP SEVENTEEN: YOUR LETTER TO YOU

Now I want you to write a letter to yourself. Not just any letter. This letter is about your hopes, dreams, goals and plans. Take your time in writing it. Pretend you are writing to a friend, someone you love and respect. Picture someone who deserves happiness and the very best in life. Imagine you are writing the letter in six weeks' time. Here's what you need to do:

* Look back over the past six weeks and appreciate yourself for what you've achieved so far.

* Remind yourself of your goals and why they are important to you.

* Give yourself warm and generous praise for your good qualities and talents.

* Ask yourself how your career plan is going and whether you've achieved the goals you set yourself to achieve by this stage.

* Give yourself encouragement to carry on, to believe in yourself and to believe in the outcome.

* Remind yourself of all the things you can do to support yourself.

When you've finished the letter, seal it and give it to someone you trust, asking him or her to post or give it to you in six weeks' time. You'll probably forget the letter between now and then. This means that, when you receive it, you'll read it in a fresh light - as if seeing it for the first time - and really absorb what it says.

It will encourage and support you, and, at the same time, it will remind you of your plans and goals, and that the way to achieve them is to keep going. It will give you an opportunity to review your progress to date and a chance to update your plans. You can see how far you've come, what you've achieved and where you need to go next. If you're slipping, it will help you to get back on track. If you're doing well, it will give you a much-deserved pat on the back.

You may decide to do this exercise again, writing another letter to yourself for six weeks later. You may even decide to write a weekly letter, updating your progress. Through letters like this, you can keep a check on how you're doing and spur yourself on to bigger and better things. They're a great way of supporting yourself. Keep them bright and cheerful, and write on lovely paper or cards.

Your letter to you is a way of valuing and encouraging yourself.

STEP EIGHTEEN: PRESENTING YOURSELF

Today, you're going to think about the way you present yourself to the world. You know yourself. You know the essential you - the warm, funny, clever, talented you. Other people who meet you for the first time know only what they see. So, it's vital for you to make sure that what they see is great and that what they hear when you speak to them backs that up and is equally great.

As you go after the career you want, you may meet people in all sorts of different situations. They may be prospective bosses or employers, colleagues, clients, patients or business partners. They may be people you admire and respect, or people you know nothing about. Everyone, no matter how important or unimportant you think they are, counts. They should go away with a good impression of you. So today I want you to give yourself an honest all-over review and to check whether anything needs updating, improving or changing.

Hair
Your hair should be clean and well cut, whatever your style.

Face
If you wear make-up, keep it subtle during the daytime. Learn how to flatter your looks and accentuate your best features.

Clothes
Your clothes should look smart, but should never be overwhelming. You want people to remember you, not what you were wearing. Be true to your own style, but, if it's flamboyant, tone it down in formal situations.

Jewellery
The same principles apply as with your clothes. Don't go over the top with anything too loud or showy, especially during the day.

Body
Don't wear very strong perfume. Light, refreshing, subtle scents are best.

The impression people should take away is of someone who is clean, fresh and stylish. A woman who knows what she likes and has good taste, and whose looks back up her personality.

Behaviour is the next key area. Here are the basic rules:

Listen
Never butt in or act as if you know it all. Listen to what people have to say.

Ask
If something's not clear, don't be afraid to ask about it.

Speak up
Don't whisper, giggle or say "um" too many times. Make your point clearly and directly.

Say what you think
Don't try to flatter people or give the answer you think they want. That will only irritate them! Be you, say what you think and be prepared to back it up and say why.

Look straight
Looking at the floor, out of the window or over someone's shoulder is another irritating habit. It often stems from shyness, but it's better to stop yourself doing it and look the other person in the eye. Not defiantly, simply pleasantly.

Emphasize your good points and strengths. Don't worry about the things you cannot change. Concentrate on giving the best of yourself and you'll be a star.

Whatever the career you plan, presenting yourself well is important.

STEP NINETEEN: LOOK FOR ENERGIZERS

Wherever you go in life and whatever you do, you'll come across two kinds of people: the drainers and the energizers. Of course, there are people who don't fall neatly into either category. These two categories are the ones to look out for, however, as they can both have a strong influence over your working life.

Here's how you recognize the two types:

Drainers

* Leave you feeling drained after you've spent time with them.

* Often present themselves as victims.

* May at first have you feeling sorry for them, but this sympathy will eventually turn to irritation.

* Never do anything positive to make their lives better.

* Ask you for advice as a way of telling you all their troubles and getting you involved in them.

* Never act on the advice you offer.

* Stay stuck in their work, relationships, etc.

* Have no real interest in you, your work or your life.

* Have no insight - they can't understand why things go wrong for them.

* Will take up your time, your energy and your effort and give nothing back.

Energizers

* Leave you feeling good and raring to go.

* Present themselves as competent, capable and effective.

* Bring out the best in you.

* Invite admiration, respect and friendship.

* Take responsibility for their lives.

* Ask your opinion and respect it, acting on it at times.

* Are always moving forwards in life, work and relationships.

* Show genuine interest in you and know how to form real friendships.

* Possess genuine insight, but never force it on others.

* Give more than they take in any relationship.

It's very clear from these lists that drainers are people to be avoided whenever possible, and energizers are people to seek out. If you can't avoid drainers, keep contact to a minimum, and never invest your time and energy in them. Don't bother suggesting solutions to their problems or nodding sympathetically - just get on with whatever you're doing. Drainers are drawn like magnets to anyone who'll listen.

Energizers, on the other hand, are very attractive and are the people to be around and to learn from. Energizers tend to rise to the top, to be successful without being arrogant and to be fun while getting a lot done. Your working life will always be richer for the presence of an energizer or two.

Energizers are the people who make things happen - be one yourself.

STEP TWENTY: TAKING RISKS

It's time to think about the risk-taking involved in going after your dream career. Why? Because when you knock on doors, you take risks. When you ask for help, apply for jobs and courses, or reach for the top, you take risks. In other words, risks are an inevitable part of moving on and aiming for the best.

The only way to avoid risks is by playing it utterly safe, which means staying put, sticking with what you have and accepting boredom and frustration. It is the easy option, but gets you nowhere. Risk-taking, when it's carefully considered and is part of making wise choices, is exciting and exhilarating. Sure, you risk losing, failing or being told no, but you also risk finding, succeeding, joy, fulfilment and satisfaction.

WHEN SHOULD YOU TAKE A RISK?

When the potential good outcome outweighs the potential loss. That is, when what you want is important enough for you to go for it and take a chance on losing. If you want that job, that deal, that meeting badly enough, you put everything you have into getting it and trust you'll have the right outcome. If you lose, you try again. If you succeed, you feel fantastic. And that high, that feeling of exhilaration when everything works out and comes together, is worth the risk-taking.

A life lived safely is a flat life, a life without energy or passion. Risk-taking is not a bad thing. It's a choice to make if you want to move beyond your comfort zone - beyond what feels easy, familiar and comfortable to you. If you want to have your dream career, you must be brave enough to venture into new pastures and take chances.

TAKING RISKS

Ask yourself what risks you would take and what risks you would steer clear of? Which outcomes would you be willing to accept and which would you rather avoid? When is a risk exciting and motivating, and when does it become too scary?

Get to know your personal risk level. For instance, you may be willing to risk being turned down for the job you really want, but not be willing to risk losing your present job. Decide what feels comfortable to you, what your comfort zone is, then push yourself a little beyond it. For instance, if your comfort zone allows you to apply for another job which sounds okay, but not the one you really dream of, take the risk, go further and apply for the one you truly want.

Take wise risks and be a winner in life.

STEP TWENTY-ONE: THE TRUTH ABOUT FAILURE

The time has come for you to look at the part failure plays in your working life. The biggest single factor which stops people succeeding, fulfilling their dreams and having the careers they really want is fear of failure. Fear of failure is paralyzing. It stops you standing tall, taking chances and aiming for the top.

'Who am I to do that?" people ask themselves. "I'm just little ol' me, I'm never going to get to the top." Why not?

The people who get to the top and achieve what they want in life are not always more talented, more able, cleverer than everybody else. Often they're simply braver. They may fear failure, but they face their fears and push on anyway.

Overcome your fear of failure and you need overcome nothing else.

People who succeed have frequently failed first. There is no big success without failure. Most very successful people have failed many times along the way.

Here's a story about failure: Some years ago, an elderly man in the USA, who had just retired, decided that the best thing he had going for him was his chicken recipe and that he would sell it. He went to a food outlet and offered the recipe for a share in the profits. The owners told him to forget it. But he kept trying until he'd been turned away 1,008 times. On the 1,009th try, his recipe was accepted. His name was Colonel Sanders, and so began Kentucky Fried Chicken.

If he'd given up after 1,008 failures, he would never have succeeded. Some of the most famous books in the world have been turned down by many publishers before being accepted. Many people wrote off Jennifer Capriati when her personal life and tennis fell apart, but she fought back to become the world's number one women's player. Richard Dyson tried many, many times before he invented the bagless vacuum cleaner. Look around, and you'll see many more examples.

People who succeed keep on trying. They believe in themselves, and they learn from their failures.

Ask yourself today:

* What have my failures been so far?

* What can I learn from them?

* Am I willing to go for what I want and take failure in my stride?

* Will I believe in myself even when it seems that no one else will?

....

....

....

....

....

....

Every failure has a part to play in your journey to success. So don't fear failure - simply take it in your stride.

Failure is the price
you pay for success.

STEP TWENTY-TWO: BE REALISTIC

Now think about how realistic your plans and ambitions are. I use the word realistic with great care. Mostly when people ask, "Are you being realistic?" they're trying to put a damper on what you're doing. "Be realistic" can sound like a put-down, as if the person who says it thinks you're chasing dreams which you can't live out or overestimating your abilities. There are so many sayings that imply that you had better downscale your dreams, damp down your plans and get back to the real - for this, read tough and hostile - world.

Well, that's not the kind of realistic I mean. In the real world, people do wonderful, glorious and unexpected things every day. In the real world, people succeed despite the odds and despite people's expectations to the contrary. In the real world, dreams can come true thanks to a little talent and a lot of determination.

Here's what I mean by being realistic:

* Are you going after a career which really feels right for you?

* Have you allowed for the time you need to train/study/learn new skills?

* Is your goal one that you truly believe you can achieve, even if it takes time and effort to get there?

If you find yourself saying: "I'm just being realistic", you're probably giving yourself an excuse for being overcautious, lazy or scared. The realistic truth is that you can achieve more than you imagine you can. Whatever you think you can do, whatever you decide your upper limit is, you can be sure it is too modest. The realistic truth is that you can always do more, push yourself that little bit further and end up with something special.

We all have it in us to achieve great things. This isn't an ability given to some people and not to others. Success is there for the taking - provided that you believe you can win it and that you put in the effort.

If people tell you to "get real" or "be more realistic", by all means consider whether they have a point and whether any adjustment is needed to your plans as you move forwards. But never let anyone put you down or stop you. When you've achieved your dream, those same people will probably be saying: "I knew you could do it." The truth, however, will actually be that YOU knew you could do it - and that's why you made it.

Today and every day tell yourself: "I know I can do it. I'm living my dream. Nothing need stand in my way. I know myself and I trust myself to get me where I want to go."

Be realistic and have the career you were meant for.

STEP TWENTY-THREE: WORK VERSUS HOME

This is the point where I want you to look at the balance between your working life and your home life. On your way to the career of your dreams, this is something you need to get right from the start - and to keep right as you progress. There are a few myths about work and about the home/work balance which need to be addressed right now.

Do you agree with any of the following statements?

☐ The harder you work, the more you'll succeed.

☐ People who work long hours are to be respected and admired.

☐ If a job's great, you shouldn't mind what hours you have to put in.

☐ To get where you want in your career, your home life has to be put on hold for a while.

☐ You can't have a great job and a great home life/relationship.

☐ A boss will always think more of you if you work extra hard and extra hours.

Take a good look at your working life now. What kind of hours are you working? Do you take proper breaks or do you feel under pressure not to and guilty if you do? Do you come in early or stay late at night to get things finished? Are you expected to work extra hours for no extra pay? If you say yes to any of these and if you agree with any of the statements above, it's time to think again. We live in a society that glorifies work and encourages employees to believe that, when it comes to work, more is better.

Here are the truths behind the myths:

* Overwork often makes people ill, tired, miserable and less effective.

* Without a proper home/work balance, it's impossible to be creative and productive in the long term.

* People who overwork are often simply avoiding another part of their lives.

* No job should take up more than eight hours a day. If you are asked or expected to work for longer than this, the company is understaffed and won't be a good one to work for.

* When it comes to work, less is often more. A few hours of really productive work are worth more than a long, tiring day of grinding chores. Freelancers soon learn this - those who work for themselves usually find that they get jobs done in half the time.

No matter how great your job, never be tempted to overwork. Your home life is important. Your partner, friends and family matter more than work ever will. No one wants "She did a good job" to be her only epitaph.

Keep the work/home balance and stay healthy and happy.

STEP TWENTY-FOUR: TAKING ACTION

Today is all about sustained action. It's important to know what you want. It's vital to have a plan and to take the first step. To make your dreams come true, however, and have the career you really want, you need to take action - AND KEEP ON TAKING IT.

Success is about taking action whether you feel like it or not. It's all too easy to have a burst of effort and then fall flat and lose your motivation. That's how most people fall by the wayside. They end up saying: "Well, I gave it a go" or "I tried, but it became too hard" or "I soon discovered that I didn't have the time/energy/nerve." Don't be one of them.

You can be an also-ran if you want to. Or you can be a winner, out there in front with the people who found the time, the energy and the nerve, day in and day out, until they succeeded.

Remember that anything is possible.

Even in a busy life there's time to go for your goals. You could:

* Get up an hour earlier than usual.

* Skip some of your less interesting socializing.

* Make time in your lunch hour.

* Put aside ten minutes a day and a whole evening once a week.

* Cut down on repetitive chores.

Once you have identified the best career for you, taking action is more important than anything else. The right beliefs are crucial, but, without action, the right beliefs won't get you that career. Take action every day. For instance:

* Make a telephone call.

* Update your plan.

* Review your presentation.

* Do more research.

* Read about the career you want.

Do anything else you need to do to keep moving forwards towards your goal. Taking action is the way to change your world. Let other people talk about what they're going to do. Save your words and take action instead. Let others look around and wonder what happened as you streak ahead of them. Enjoy the well-earned rewards that taking action will bring you.

The way to feel excited is to Take Action. The way to dispel doubts is to Take Action. The way to get results is to Take Action. The way to believe in yourself is to Take Action. The way to follow your goals is to Take Action.

Taking action is the only way to achieve the career you truly want.

STEP TWENTY-FIVE: MARKET YOURSELF

Now it's necessary to look at the way in which you market yourself. This may sound like a strange idea, but the truth is that, no matter what your career, you have to sell yourself. Every single one of us does. So it's worth putting time and effort into doing it well and making sure that you're selling the right things.

Think of yourself as a business - Me Ltd.

This is obviously essential for the self-employed, but would-be employees are also offering potential buyers (employers) products and services (their skills and talents). That's what the world of work is all about. Whether you're an artist, a computer expert, a teacher, an accountant, a beauty therapist or a stockbroker, you're selling others your unique assets.

Here are some questions to ask yourself about Me Ltd:

* What am I selling and who am I selling it to?

* What have I got to offer that's special?

* What is my advantage over the competition?

* Are my prices right?

* Is my advertisement (CV) the best it can be?

Getting these key elements right is important. Even a chance conversation at a party or in the street could lead to work you want to do.

If someone asks you: "What do you do?" never groan and tell them about your awful job. Instead, tell them about the career you're developing, whether you're actually doing it yet or not. You might say: "I'm setting up in business as an interior decorator" or "I'm training to be a reflexologist."

Don't use words such as "hope" or "might". Sound sure of yourself and as though you delight in what you do. Weeks or months down the line, that person is likely to remember you when someone else asks: "Do you know of a good decorator?" or "Can you recommend a reflexologist?"

Think of yourself as your own PR consultant. Be the advertising agency for Me Ltd, and make sure your company gets the very best publicity and that people hear only good things about it. To be successful, you must be comfortable describing what you do and what you bring to the marketplace. Most of us find it easier to talk about someone else in glowing terms. Try asking a friend to be your PR consultant and describe what you do - and how well you do it. Then try it yourself, and practise until you feel at ease doing it. It will prove extremely useful!

Learn to feel good about selling what you have to offer.

122

STEP TWENTY-SIX: COUNT EVERY SUCCESS

It's high time to count your successes. Don't think you have that many? Of course you do. Think you could count your successes on the fingers of one hand? No way! Every one of us has had hundreds of successes in our life. We just don't always notice them and give ourselves credit.

All too often, we focus on the things we got wrong, didn't manage, messed up or shrank from. We've all had those, too. But why make an issue out of them when it only makes you miserable and knocks your confidence. Instead, choose to make an issue out of your successes. Start noticing them, and appreciate yourself for them. Give yourself treats and rewards for your achievements.

SUCCESSES

Start with school, then work your way through to the present day, noting every work-related success you've had. You might include:

* Any exams you passed.

* Friendships you formed at school/college/work.

* Jobs you were offered.

* Difficult people you coped with - bullies, demanding bosses, etc.

* Projects you did well.

* Words of praise and appreciation that other people gave you.

* Ideas you put forward that were used.

* The positive way you responded to difficult challenges.

* Personal problems you overcame - anything at all, such as dyslexia or a difficult home life.

* Hurts and setbacks you put behind you.

Success isn't just measured in certificates and awards. The true measure of your success is the way you handle life's challenges and the happiness that you create in your life.

Count your successes with pride. When someone says something appreciative or complimentary to you, write it down on a piece of paper and put it in a pretty box or tin. You'll be amazed by how fast the pieces of paper in your box multiply. Those positive comments from others are just one measure of your success.

Think of yourself as a successful person. Successful people have quiet confidence - they don't boast, but they don't suffer fools either. They know their own worth, and they don't bother with false modesty. They have the glow that success brings.

Count every success and appreciate your own value.

STEP TWENTY-SEVEN: RELY ON YOURSELF

Today I want you to focus on the key area of self-reliance. Whatever job you do, whatever your dream career, it's vital that you learn to rely on yourself. Why? Because as soon as you begin to rely on other people or on institutions, you lose the potential for success and fulfilment.

In the world we live in, self-reliance is more important than it has ever been before. More and more people rely on the welfare state to support them. While welfare for those who truly need it is a wonderful thing, for many others it creates a dependency that undermines them. In the same way, depending on parents or even a partner for financial support is undermining. To feel really adult, successful and fulfilled, you need to work at something that both excites and pays you.

You need to be able to rely on yourself, no matter what. If things at work go wrong, if your plans don't work out, if you are made redundant or sacked, your self-reliance will see you through. Knowing that you can depend on yourself will mean that - whatever happens - you'll be able to cope and move on to better things.

Here's what self-reliance involves:

Approve of yourself
No matter what you look like, what you wear, what you say or don't say, make the decision today never to judge or criticize yourself unjustly - give yourself approval instead. Be honest where improvements would help - and try to make them - but be nice to yourself, notice all the good things and agree with your decisions!

Be your own best friend
Think about how you treat your closest friend, then treat yourself in the same way - with warmth, compassion, encouragement and support.

Don't moan
Never waste time and energy moaning about things that have gone wrong for you. No one benefits, least of all you. Instead, try to keep your conversations upbeat and cheerful - however hard this is at times.

Minimize problems
Deal with your problems yourself whenever possible. Make wise decisions, see problems shrinking rather than growing and always look for solutions.

Trust your judgement
You may want to ask advice from one or two close friends, but don't ask more people than that, as you're likely to receive conflicting advice and become confused. Look to yourself for answers. You're the wisest judge of what's best for you.

Practise self-reliance every day and make it a lifetime habit. It will always stand you in good stead.

Be self-reliant and know that you can cope with anything.

STEP TWENTY-EIGHT: KNOW WHEN TO JUMP

Now you need to look at when the time is right to make a major career move. If you're in a job which is lukewarm, awful or terminally boring, you're going to have to leave it in order to do a job that you will love. The question is when. Only you can judge the right time to jump, but there are indicators that will help you.

The right time may be obvious - when you have the job of your dreams lined up and can move smoothly from one to the other. In many cases, however, it doesn't work like this. You may need to move to a transition job, something that will act as a bridge and pay the bills while you progress towards the career you truly want.

Your dream job may involve going freelance. In fact, dream jobs often do, as for many people nothing is more satisfying than being their own boss and deciding on their own working rules. If you're planning to go freelance, you may be hesitating about when to make the jump.

There's no perfect time, but here's a checklist to work with:

☐ Have you lined up some work that will earn enough to keep you going while you take the next step?

☐ Are you itching to get out of where you are?

☐ Do you feel excited and energized by your plans for a new career?

☐ Have you done the research, made the contacts, got a good idea of what will be involved and made a plan?

☐ Do you trust yourself enough to know that, whatever happens, you'll cope?

If you can answer yes to all of these questions, you're ready to jump.

A note of warning: However tempting it may be to go to see your boss and tell him or her what you really feel about your job before you announce that you're leaving - don't. And don't come clean about your loathing for a colleague, either. You may experience a short-term feeling of satisfaction, but the cost may be more than you imagine. You'll leave your boss with a lasting image of you as immature and uncontrolled. Better to stay on good terms with everyone and to deal with any anger privately. You may need a good reference, or business contacts and information, to help you build your new career.

When you decide the time is right to jump, do it with dignity and humour, self-respect and foresight. Celebrate, then move on to what really matters - your new career. Jump in the right way and at the right time, and feel the thrill!

Choose when to jump and keep the power all yours.

STEP TWENTY-NINE: THIS IS FOR LIFE

This is the day to think about the rest of your working life and to remind yourself that what you are doing now is laying the foundations for the career you really deserve - a career which employs your talent and ability and which rewards you with fulfilment, challenge, fun and happiness.

Here are the guidelines I want you to work with from here on:

Always have a plan
You already know about the importance of creating a plan for moving into the career you really want. Even after you are in that career, however, it's still important to have a plan. Always know what your next goals are and how you are going to achieve them. Enjoy the present while looking ahead to the future you want to create.

Adapt your plan

Life is full of surprises, and working life is no different. Be prepared for the unexpected. Change and surprise are a part of life, yet they can feel uncomfortable and scary. Be ready to take whatever comes along in your stride, to keep cool and to adapt your plan in whatever way is necessary.

Keep on track

You may need to adapt your plan, but that doesn't mean giving up your goals. It simply means, at times, finding different ways around obstacles and new ways to move forwards. Be flexible, but never let your dreams go. Stay on track, and keep your dreams as important to you as ever.

Keep your priorities

Work deserves a prominent place in your life. What you do, how you earn your living and using your abilities well all matter. But never let work take over or be everything to you. A good life is a life in balance, a life that contains work, but also contains home, leisure, a social scene and time for you.

Keep good company

In your working life, the people you mix with are very important. Studies have shown that we are deeply influenced by those with whom we spend most of our time. We tend to think, dress and behave in a similar way. So, make sure you keep the very best company, and spend your time with people who have humour, grace, compassion, intelligence and wisdom. Let their qualities rub off on you, and avoid anyone who doesn't treat you or themselves well.

Follow these simple guidelines for the rest of your working life and you'll always know the real meaning of success. Stay true to yourself and your goals, and always treat others with compassion and respect.

Make sure your working life is always rich and rewarding.

STEP THIRTY: CELEBRATE!

Well done! You've come this far and should be very proud of yourself. Doing all the exercises in this book will have meant working hard, thinking a lot about your qualities and what you want in life, and putting energy and effort into bringing what you want into your life.

Now it's time to celebrate. Do this in any way that most appeals to you: a glass of champagne, a night out, a party, a treat for yourself - or all of them! Celebrating is a way of appreciating:

* You and your talents.

* Your good fortune, in whatever shape or form it has arrived.

* The people who've helped and supported you.

* Your achievements so far.

* The excitement of knowing what you really want to do.

* The knowledge that, if you're not doing it quite yet, you're on your way and will be doing it very soon.

* Your courage and motivation.

* Your willingness to take risks and go for what you want.

* The pleasure there is to be found in working at something that you love doing.

* The fact that you can love your work AND earn plenty of money.

* The knowledge that you'll always keep your working life in balance with the rest of your life.

* Knowing that you can cope with any obstacles you may encounter.

Celebrate all of this and congratulate yourself - you deserve to. Remember, though, that, while it's great to celebrate all your achievements and all that's good in your life, a little humility is an important part of success. Here are some maxims to remember in your working life that will ensure your success is not at the expense of others or of your own good judgement:

* Enjoy your achievements but never grow complacent.

* Appreciate what you have and never take anything for granted.

* Value those around you, and never talk down to anyone.

* Always keep your affairs in order, and never do anything dishonest.

* Be proud of what you do, but never boast.

* Be fair, be open and be straight in your dealings with everyone you come across.

* Trust your instincts, but make sensible checks as well to confirm them.

Let this be your guide as you go on to future success, and enjoy every step you take along the way.

Celebrate -
you deserve to
feel fantastic!

A FINAL WORD

Now it's time for the rest of your working life to begin and for you to go on to the career success that you so richly deserve. Remember that you already have everything you need inside you. The courage, motivation and determination to have a brilliant career are already yours.

Be true to yourself and you will always do the work that is right for you. Never accept anything less. To work at something which has no meaning for you or which you dislike can grind you down. Remind yourself that there is always the possibility for change and that you can reach out for what you want to do.

Never let self-doubt hold you back. Doubts and fears are there to be confronted and overcome. Be the kind of person who never lets life's obstacles get in the way. Be one of life's winners, and pass your success on to others, showing them that career success can be theirs as well and giving them encouragement to rise to the challenge.

Work well, work hard,
work wisely and
enjoy yourself!

DATING

You deserve to find real love. You deserve a warm, exciting, funny, sexy, generous, committed and loving relationship with a man who appreciates, respects and loves you.

It doesn't matter how old or young you are, whether you've been in lots of relationships or none at all, whether you always end it or he does, whether you rush in or go at snail's pace, whether you know why you haven't found love so far or you don't have a clue - none of these things matters. Love is still only an arm's reach away from you.

All that is truly important is that you know that you want love and that you are willing to put some time and energy into finding it and bringing it into your life.

Finding love isn't just a question of luck. You can wait for it, like a princess in a tower waiting for her knight. Or you can make the changes, put in the effort and go out and find it. Which would you rather do? Wait, not knowing whether it will ever come? Or go out and find it, knowing that if you do you cannot fail.

If you're open and willing, I will show you, step by step, what you need to do. In 30 days you can transform your world and make changes you never imagined possible. The path to finding love is an exciting one and with each step you take you will feel love draw ever closer.

Decide to find love and let the adventure begin . . .

"WHAT WOULD YOU DO IF YOU WEREN'T AFRAID?"

SHERYL SANDBERG

STEP ONE: ARE YOU READY?

You want a relationship, right? And not just any relationship - a fantastic one. An exciting, lasting, passionate and fun relationship with a man who's open, honest, understanding and supportive. Not to mention solvent, responsible and grown-up enough to have his own life pretty well sorted out.

Sounds good, doesn't it? You've waited long enough, made enough mistakes, kissed enough frogs - now you're ready for real love with the right person. And you're going to find it, if you're determined, brave and honest with yourself. It's time for the first step towards finding love, and that is to check just how ready you are. It's all very well being ready in principle. It's fine to talk about finding love, to wish, to hope and to dream. Being truly ready to take the first step, however, means being willing to take action, to make changes and to do things differently. That can feel uncomfortable and a little scary. Sometimes it's a lot easier just to go on talking about what you want, rather than actually doing what's needed to bring it into your life.

Today I want you to think about the following key points and to prepare yourself for the changes you're about to make in your life:

* Are you ready to shed your excuses, outdated beliefs and unhelpful attitudes that keep you stuck in the same old patterns and prevent you having what you want?

* Are you ready to think in new ways, adopt new beliefs and become the kind of person who can attract the love you want in your life?

* Are you ready to take action and to keep taking action until you succeed?

* Are you ready to be open to change, however uncomfortable it may feel, and to welcome new possibilities into your life?

* Are you ready to give love, to be loved and to share your life with another person?

Think hard about every one of these questions. What will it mean for you to share your space, your way of life, your inner thoughts and feelings? If you want to find real love, this is precisely what it will involve.

EXERCISE

Say to yourself out loud: "I am ready for love." See how it feels. Repeat this phrase throughout the day. Notice the prickles of excitement, the moments of fear and the shivers of anticipation it may evoke. When you can say it standing in front of a mirror and looking yourself right in the eye, meaning it with all your heart, you're ready to start the journey to the kind of relationship that you want.

You are ready for love and all that it will bring you.

STEP TWO: REMOVING THE BLOCKS

Before you can go out and find love, you have to remove any blocks that you may have put in its path.

Imagine yourself looking out of the window at a beautiful little garden just across the road. There are lush green plants, exquisite flowers, a small pond with a waterfall, and in the middle a seat where you long to sit, soaking in the beauty and magic of the surroundings. To get there, however, you need to navigate a path that is littered with obstacles: concrete blocks, heaps of rubble, piles of rotting garbage and discarded pieces of machinery. It looks daunting, but you want to reach the garden so much that you set out to make your way past all the obstacles.

Some of the impediments are surprisingly easy to remove - you can simply lift them out of the way. Others are heavy and stubbornly refuse to be moved. You have to try harder, take a little longer. But in the end you do it. The path is clear and you make it to the garden.

The blocks in life are exactly the same as the obstacles on the way to the garden. Whether we put them there ourselves or whether other people have placed them in our way isn't important. Just say to yourself that any block, no matter how big or how heavy, can be removed.

What are the blocks on your path to finding love? You may know some straight away. Others may be harder to identify.

The blocks on your path to finding love could be lifestyle choices, attitudes, other people around you or the way you feel about yourself. You may not even have realized that there are blocks there. Now that you know they exist, you can work at identifying them and start to move them out of your way.

Here are some examples:

* You hardly ever go out because you hate parties, bars and clubs, so your chances of meeting someone are pretty low.

* You refuse to make having a relationship a priority and place more importance on everything else in your life.

* You allow your mum/dad/best friend to tell you who you should or shouldn't date.

* You go out with anyone who asks you just because you're so grateful to be asked. This means you often spend your time with men who are wrong for you.

* You don't go out with anyone because you're shy, convinced you're ugly or scared of getting involved.

* You'd rather talk about how lovely it would be to have a great relationship than DO anything about it.

Get the idea?

How do you move these blocks? By recognizing them, deciding to shift them and then taking the necessary steps to do this, whatever those may be. You may need to start accepting invitations, to prioritize finding a relationship, to ask your best friend to take more of a back seat in your love life or to start making choices that are right for you. You'll know what needs doing once you know what the blocks are.

> Remove the blocks and let love into your life.

STEP THREE: NO MORE EXCUSES

This is the day when you're going to clear out all the stale old excuses that you've been using for not having a great relationship. No matter how badly you may want a relationship, if it's not in your life now it's because you've been clinging to excuses for not having it. Before you can go ahead and find the right relationship, you have to spring-clean your mind of all the buts, ifs and maybes you've been using to avoid it.

Why do we use excuses? Because they are a way of keeping things safely as they are now. Even if you think you don't like things as they are now, the situation is what you're used to and so it's comfortable and familiar to stick with the status quo. Also, a part of you prefers it that way, the part that's scared of change and of the various challenges a relationship will bring - to know someone really intimately; to share your space, time and possessions; and to really open up to another person.

Dumping your excuses will mean pulling the rug out from under the reluctant part of yourself. It will give the green light to the bigger part of you that's excited about getting out there and finding the love you want and deserve.

What are your excuses?

Spend five minutes writing down all the excuses you use to avoid a relationship. You should end up with between five and ten.

Here are some favourite ones:

* I'm simply too busy to meet anyone . . .

* My life's great as it is - a relationship would be just a nice extra.

* I'm always attracted to the wrong type.

* I'm still not over the big hurt.

* I've got to lose weight/give up smoking/move house first.

* I'm concentrating on my career at the moment.

* Whenever I meet someone I like, he's already taken.

* My hands are full with the kids/my mum/my sister.

* Men/women are always intimidated by my success.

* No one would want to take on someone as difficult as me.

Recognize anything? You may find some of your excuses listed here, or you may come up with completely different ones. Just be sure to get them all down on paper.

Well done! That's got them out into the open and labelled as what they are: excuses that stop you from having a fantastic relationship.

Now it's time to bin them, once and for all.

EXERCISE

Pick a quiet time to do this exercise. Make sure there won't be any interruptions, and lie or sit somewhere comfortable with your eyes closed:

Imagine that the excuses you've identified are hanging around your neck on chains, weighing you down like heavy stones. You can hardly move under the sheer weight of them and you're desperate to off-load the burden.

Gradually, with enormous effort, you manage to lift them, one by one, from your neck and drop them into a sack. When they're all off, you rub your stiff neck and stretch your aching back, then drag the sack across to a huge black pit. You shove the sack into the pit and watch it fall to the bottom.

You then walk away and, as you do so, you feel your body lightening and your energy returning. Your shoulders straighten up and a sense of joy and excitement fills you until you want to run, dance and leap in the air. You're free.

Now open your eyes and savour the sense of freedom you have just created. This is your starting point, your launch pad for finding the relationship you want. You have a clean slate, a fresh start, a whole new beginning.

From now on, your old excuses are gone. They're hollow, empty and meaningless. If you find yourself resorting to any one of them again - to yourself or to anyone else - stop immediately and say to yourself:

I am completely
free to find the
relationship I want.

STEP FOUR: ROOT OUT NEGATIVE BELIEFS

In this step you're going to look at your relationship beliefs and decide which ones are useful and which ones need changing. We all gather beliefs as we grow up. Some come from our parents, some from family members, teachers and friends. Others come from what we see in the world around us. We take on certain beliefs and then behave as though they're absolute truths, rigid and unchangeable.

Once we have certain beliefs, we look for evidence to support them in the world around us. Every time you see, hear or read something that fits in with one of your beliefs, it confirms it for you even more deeply.

Your beliefs are incredibly powerful. They govern your thoughts, which in turn govern your actions.

In order to find the love you are looking for, you need to get rid of negative and unhelpful beliefs. If you don't, however hard you try, you won't attract the person you want into your life - or you'll make sure that you lose them as fast as possible. You'll then resort to your beliefs to justify what happened, simply compounding them and ingraining them more deeply into your attitudes to life and love . . .

You will tell yourself: "I knew I couldn't hang on to someone nice" or "No one wants to be with me".

The wonderful thing about beliefs is that, far from being unalterable, they can in fact be changed in a remarkably short space of time. Although children may have little choice about what they're taught to believe, adults can choose their own beliefs. This means that the power for change is in your hands.

EXERCISE

The first step is to identify the negative beliefs that have been holding you back. Take ten minutes to write down as many as you can. You may find some of your beliefs on the following list and you will almost certainly be able to come up with a few more of your own.

Here are some examples:

* I'm not attractive.

* I don't deserve love.

* I always get dumped.

* I grow bored with partners so quickly that I have to dump them.

* I make the wrong choices.

* I can find partners, but I can't keep them.

* I don't know how to let anyone get close to me.

....

....

....

....

....

....

....

Once you have finished your list, go through it and examine each of your beliefs. Are they really true? Or is each one something you have chosen to believe because of things that have happened in the past? Perhaps someone hurt you. Painful though that was, it hasn't been your only experience and needn't form the basis of your beliefs for the future. Perhaps a cruel remark stuck and became a rigidly held belief about yourself. But there will have been other kind and appreciative remarks. Why stick with the nasty one?

Decide now that you will let these negative beliefs go and choose not to embrace them any longer. They are old, tired, burdensome and outdated.

Let go of negative beliefs and set yourself free.

STEP FIVE: CHOOSE YOUR NEW BELIEFS

Now that you've rooted out your longstanding negative and damaging beliefs, here comes the fun part - choosing the beliefs that you really want to have.

Before you begin it's important to recognize that you do already have plenty of useful, good and supportive beliefs, as well as those negative and restrictive old ones. Spend ten minutes writing down all the positive beliefs you have about yourself and relationships.

Here are some examples:

* I'm trustworthy and loyal.

* I know a good person when I meet one.

* I'm fun to be with and good company.

* I'm generous.

* I'm great at sharing.

* I won't be put down or trampled upon.

* I pick myself up quickly after setbacks.

* I can talk about my feelings.

* I'm thoughtful and caring.

* It is possible to have a longlasting, fulfilling relationship.

....

....

....

....

Pick the positive beliefs that apply to you and add as many others as you can think of. Don't hold back when it comes to praising yourself: list every good quality you believe you have - and have fun doing it. Are you surprised by how many there are? This only goes to show how we tend to tuck these beliefs away deep inside, instead of bringing them out and enjoying them.

Now it's time to choose some new beliefs, which will reinforce and support those you already hold. New beliefs can be taken up surprisingly quickly; in fact we often learn them instantly.

If you doubt this, simply bring to mind any fact you have read or heard in the past 24 hours. It could be something you heard on the television news or read in a newspaper or magazine. You believed it and it is now a part of your belief system - the way you shape and make sense of the world. Why did you believe it so easily? Because you trusted the source, you were open to the belief and it made sense to you. Teaching yourself to adhere to new beliefs can happen in the same way.

EXERCISE

Make a list of five new beliefs that would be useful to you in finding a happy relationship. For instance:

* Everyone deserves a good relationship.

* People like me find love all the time.

* There are plenty of potential partners out there.

* It is possible to have a great job, lots of success and a strong relationship, too.

Use any of these plus some that you
create yourself. Now take your new
beliefs and learn them by heart.
Repeat them to yourself as often as
you can, especially when you find
your thoughts heading towards your
former negative beliefs.

_Choose to believe that
a great relationship
is on the way._

STEP SIX: LOOK FOR THE EVIDENCE

Today you're going to begin looking for evidence to back up your newly
adopted beliefs. Why? Because we all look for evidence to support our
beliefs every single day, without even realizing that this is what we
are doing. So if you want to change your beliefs, it's important to look
for the right evidence.

For example, your old, negative belief may be: "You can't have a great job
and a happy relationship."

Without even realizing it, you will have looked for evidence to support
this viewpoint - in books, magazines and newspapers; on television and
radio; in advertisements and in the things people around you say. Every
time you came across a woman with a great relationship but a miserable
job, or a great job but no relationship, you'll have thought to yourself:
"Ah, you see - I was right about that." Your belief will have been
cemented in even more deeply.

This is how we support ourselves in what we believe. On top of this,
because we want to be right in our beliefs, we often filter out any
contradicting evidence. You may have read a story in a newspaper about

a woman with a fabulous job but a miserable love life and ignored another story in the same newspaper about a woman with a wonderful job and a wonderful relationship.

That's why I want you to look for evidence to support your new beliefs.

Suppose your new belief is: "You can have it all - a great job and a wonderful man."

Now begin looking for evidence to support this belief, rather than dismissing it as an exception. Notice stories and examples of women proving this - there are plenty of them around! Write them down or cut out the articles and keep them. You'll soon find that you have collected a substantial bundle of "evidence"; if you need to shore up your new belief, you can simply run through it for reassurance and validation.

A national newspaper once printed a story saying that it was easier for a woman over the age of 35 to go to the moon than for her to marry. Countless numbers of unmarried women over 35 probably took this to heart and used it to confirm that they would never marry. Yet women over 35 marry ALL THE TIME: there are examples in the newspapers every day. So the statistic, as statistics can be, was misleading. There are always statistics available that you can manipulate to prove anything you want to prove.

Believe what you want to believe and then begin to notice how often your belief is true in the world around you. Build your beliefs by building the evidence that supports them.

The evidence that a great relationship is possible is all around you.

STEP SEVEN: CHANGING YOUR PATTERN

Now it's time to identify your relationship pattern, decide how useful it has been to you and what changes you'd like to make.

Everyone who has had relationships has a pattern that they fall into often without being conscious of doing so. This pattern is based on their style of behaviour in and around relationships. Here are some examples:

* You rush into one relationship after another. Each time you think "This is it!" and feel wonderful, only to decide you were wrong and dump the other person within weeks.

* You are very careful about who you get involved with and so cautious that you hardly trust anyone and take a long, long time to feel comfortable enough to date someone new.

* You just never seem to meet anyone. You can go for long periods without a relationship and most of the time this doesn't bother you too much.

* You always get hurt. Each time you think you've met a decent person, he turns out to be the kind who doesn't want to commit.

* You were so badly burned by a relationship once that you can't face trying again.

* You're critical of everyone who wants to date you. You think they cannot possibly be interesting.

* You have no confidence in yourself and hang around in the background at parties and clubs, assuming that no one will be interested in you.

Is your relationship pattern here? Probably, as almost everyone who's not in a long-term relationship fits one of these patterns. If yours is different, however, just write it down. If identifying it feels hard, think about your past few relationships or near-relationships and ask yourself what happened to make them go wrong.

Now that you know what your pattern is, you can resolve to change it. Think about the qualities and behaviour you'll need in order to establish your new pattern. Do you need to be more trusting, more open, or should you be more cautious and go more slowly? Do you need to say no more often, to get to know someone better before getting involved or to trust your own judgment more?

Decide today that you will establish a new pattern for yourself - one that leads to a healthy, lasting relationship with someone you love and respect.

Your new relationship pattern will bring you love.

STEP EIGHT: GREAT SELF-TALK

The time has come to look at the way you talk to yourself about yourself and relationships. What kind of language do you use when you talk inside your head about how your love life is going, what you want from the relationship and about what you have to offer?

Do you put yourself down, use all kinds of critical phrases and imagine that other people are doing a whole lot better than you are? Do you punish yourself for the mistakes you make and constantly tell yourself that you should do things better or perhaps differently? If so, then it is no great surprise that you haven't yet found the love you deserve. Unkind talk - your own as much as others - is demoralizing and diminishes your confidence. How can you walk out through your front door feeling sexy and attractive if you have been busy putting yourself down?

Educators now know that if you want a child to succeed, you must praise that child. Criticism will only create a badly behaved, miserable child. It is absolutely no different when you are an adult! And it makes no difference who is doing the criticizing. A put-down is a put-down, even if you're the only person who ever hears it.

EXERCISE

To discover how you talk to yourself, spend today noticing everything you say to yourself. Write some of it down, if you can. Catch yourself every time you're having a mental conversation with yourself, whether it is in the bathroom, on the way to work, when walking upstairs, while cooking a meal or when doing the washing up.

* What tone of voice do you use?

* How frequently do you use critical words or phrases?

* How often do you tell yourself that you should have done something better?

* How often do you boss yourself about?

* Do you ever use praise, kind words or a soft tone towards yourself?

The chances are that you've found you're pretty tough on yourself. Most people are critical towards themselves 90 per cent of the time. And that's no fun, is it?

If you want to attract a wonderful relationship into your life, it's time to begin being nice to yourself. The way you talk to yourself is the most important way you can do that. Once you are kind, supportive and understanding towards yourself, you'll be amazed by how quickly you start to feel good about who and what you are. When you feel good about yourself, you smile more and you become instantly more confident and attractive, so that other people will be drawn to you like a magnet.

Here's how to begin talking to yourself in an encouraging way:

* Catch yourself every time you're saying something nasty, bossy or critical to yourself.

* Replace what you're saying with something else that is appreciative, kind and understanding.

* Praise yourself for everything you do well during the day, even little things such as getting to work on time or eating something healthy.

* Smile at yourself every time you pass a mirror.

* Before you go to sleep at night, list all your good points and achievements.

Great self-talk leads to great self-esteem.

STEP NINE: BACKING YOURSELF

This is the day when all the work you've done so far comes together and you decide that from now on you will back yourself, in every possible way, in finding the relationship you truly want.

All too often we don't really back ourselves at all. We criticize and undermine ourselves and forget to give ourselves support, understanding or a pat on the back when we do well. From now on, however, you're going to be someone who supports herself through thick and thin, who hangs on in there when the going gets tough and who never lets herself down.

How do you back yourself 100 per cent? By taking these steps:

* Always be your own cheerleader.

* Support yourself in the decisions you make and stand up for yourself when others try to put you down.

* Listen to yourself.

* Decide what your opinion is in any given situation and then respect that opinion as valuable and right for you.

* Trust your judgment.

* Do what feels right for you and trust yourself to know best, even if those around you don't agree.

* Give yourself credit for your achievements, your courage, the effort you put in and the great qualities that you possess.

* Recognize your abilities and talents. You will have many of these - everyone does - and you demonstrate them every day, whether you realize it or not.

Think about situations in which you have backed yourself and trusted your judgment, then think about others in which you haven't. Remember how good it felt to back yourself and promise that you'll never let yourself down again.

Backing yourself 100 per cent is vital to finding a lasting relationship because, in choosing someone to become deeply involved with, you will need to trust yourself implicitly and know that you are capable of doing what's right for you.

If your trust in yourself and your judgment are undermined or destroyed - whether by others or by yourself - how can you know that you've met a worthwhile, trustworthy partner who will be right for you? Believe in yourself, back yourself and let it be your own good judgment that decides what, and who, is right for you.

Back yourself and
know how valuable
you really are.

STEP TEN: USE MAGIC

Today you're going to have fun using the power of magic to support your quest to find the perfect relationship for you. Lovers have used magic throughout history. It can be employed to attract the love you want and to draw into your life the person you can love and who can love you.

You don't believe in magic? That's not a problem, as it works whether you believe in it or not. All you have to be willing to do is to suspend your disbelief and give it a try. Magic is about using universal energy on your behalf, and, as long as the magic you practise is intended for the benefit of all, the universe will cooperate and contrive to bring you what you wish for.

Of course, it's important that you do all the other things necessary to secure the relationship you want. Changing your beliefs, dumping your excuses, summoning the courage to go out into the world and look for the person you want are all vital. But using a little white magic is a great way to back up all your efforts and to add universal energy and power to your personal energy.

Here's a white magic ritual you can practise daily:

Stand beside an open window or door, and cup one of your hands. Look into your cupped palm and visualize yourself with your ideal partner, in a happy relationship. Don't use a specific person, even if there's someone on whom you've got your eye. Simply imagine a warm, loving and attractive person, with his or her arms around you.

Now, with your other hand, pluck an imaginary golden thread from the air above you. Use it to sew your cupped palm, containing your dream, shut.

Grasp the end of the golden thread between the thumb and forefinger of your closed palm. Holding this thread, open your palm and throw your dream up into the sky.

Take the end of the thread that you are still holding, tuck it into your waistband and pat it three times. The universe will receive your dream and, because you still have the end of the thread, will know to whom to send it back ... fulfilled.

Another magic ritual you can try is to write out a description of your ideal partner on a piece of paper, then roll it up and tie it with a red ribbon. When the next full moon comes, bury the rolled-up paper in your back garden (or a flowerpot on a windowsill), while visualizing the love you want.

Use these and any other white magic spells or rituals that you may come across to draw love closer to you. Have fun with them - this magic is meant to be light-hearted and exciting, not gloomy and intense.

Let the power of magic draw love to you.

STEP ELEVEN: WATCH WHAT YOU SAY

Now it's time to take notice of the way you talk to other people about your relationships, or lack of them. Do you habitually point out your mistakes and seem gloomy about your chances of finding someone right? If so, it's time to stop.

People believe what you tell them and they feed those beliefs back to you. If you keep telling other people that you just can't find the right person, that you don't really need anyone or that you mess up every relationship you have, then that's what you'll hear, too. All of which will only confirm your negativity and leave you feeling convinced that your chances are hopeless.

Thoughts and words convey energy, either negative or positive. This energy has an effect on everyone around you, so it's vital that you give out positive energy. Life often gives you what you ask for. What you talk about and think about is what you're asking life for. Always be careful of what you think and say, as it tends to be what you'll get.

Try this checklist. When you're talking to friends about relationships, do you say any of the following?

☐ I'm hopeless at relationships.

☐ I always pick people who hurt me.

☐ I just know I'm heading for another disaster.

☐ I have really bad judgment when it comes to relationships.

☐ I don't understand what I do wrong.

☐ I'm afraid to try again.

☐ It would be nice to meet someone, but I'm not bothered if I don't.

☐ I'm just too choosy, I guess.

Note the phrases that sound familiar and add any more that you regularly use. These are the messages you've been sending out to your friends and to life about what you want!

Now think about the message you'd really like to be giving out. What is it that you truly want? Try some of the following statements:

* I'd love to meet someone genuinely nice.

* I feel sure that my next relationship will work out.

* I'm ready for a great relationship.

* There are lots of lovely, available people out there.

* I've learned a great deal from my past mistakes.

* Life's great, and it will be even better when I have a really good relationship.

* Being hurt will never put me off trying again.

* I have a feeling that I'm going to meet someone very soon.

* Having a wonderful relationship is extremely important to me.

Pick the ones that feel right, add
your own and use them - frequently.
The people around you - and life -
will hear what you want and it will
soon arrive on your doorstep.

Be brave and
talk about the
relationship
you really want.

STEP TWELVE: SEEK OUT SUPPORTERS

Right, this is it. It's time to think about the people you spend the most
time with and how much they support you in finding the relationship
you want and deserve.

All the effort you're making and all the backing you're giving
yourself will be useless if you're spending a lot of time with people
who undermine or discourage you. This can often be so subtle that
it's difficult to spot. Friends and family may be well meaning in the
things they say, but they can still leave you feeling miserable, however
unintentionally. Sometimes, too, people aren't well meaning. They're
simply jealous or unhappy, and they dump these feelings onto you by
putting you down.

Watch out for:

* People who sympathize with you yet at the same time agree that
  you're not likely to find relationship happiness.

* People who tell you that no one would ever love or accept you
  as you are.

* People who treat you like a loser in love and joke about it.

* People who leave you feeling criticized or undermined, even if you're not exactly sure why.

* People who are generally negative and gloomy.

If there are people like this in your life, make a decision to spend less time with them while you're looking for a relationship. Back away gently, and keep contact to a minimum. When you do see them, don't talk about relationships.

Instead, look out for:

* People who are warm and enthusiastic about your chances of finding real love.

* People who encourage and support you in genuine ways.

* People who are positive in their outlook on life.

* People who you feel really like and appreciate you.

* People who don't consider you a threat to their own relationships or treat you as a fifth wheel.

Think about people you know who are like this and how much contact you have with them. Do you need to strengthen your relationships with supportive people? If so, make the first move RIGHT NOW. Call and arrange to see a friend like this, ask someone supportive out for a drink, or talk to an old friend whom you haven't seen for a while. Put your energy into the people who support you.

Make sure that you spend as much time as possible with people like this and really enjoy their support and encouragement. These are the people to trust with your hopes and dreams, and to confide in when you need to talk.

Good people leave you feeling good.

STEP THIRTEEN: YOUR SHOPPING LIST

Prepare to have fun. Today you're going to draw up a shopping list of all the qualities you'd like in a perfect partner. You can indulge yourself totally, get as carried away as you want and put absolutely anything on your list - no matter how outrageous, insignificant or hilarious it may be.

But there's a serious side to this, too. Until you have a really clear idea of who your ultimate partner would be, you will never be able to judge whether potential partners you meet come close to this ideal, or you are on the right track. Once you know exactly what you want, you'll be able to decide, very quickly, whether it's worth pursuing possible relationships that come your way.

I'm not suggesting that only your ideal in every respect will do. Like everyone else in the world, you'll need to compromise on some points. It will be up to you, however, to decide where you will compromise and where you won't, what truly matters and what you can overlook or let go of.

EXERCISE

Grab a pen or pencil and settle down for half an hour on your own. It's tempting to do this one with friends and have a laugh. Don't. They'll distract you and make suggestions, and this needs to come from you and you alone. After all, you're the one who is going to be with this person. Now make a list under each heading. Put down only things that matter to you, but be honest about what matters. Don't dismiss anything as too trivial. If you hate smoking, then it's fine to put "nonsmoker" on your list of requirements.

Character

Qualities ....
....
....

Looks ....
....
....

Habits ....
....
....

Beliefs ....
....
....

Skills and Talents ....
....
....

Family and Friends ....
....
....

Hopes and Dreams ....
....
....
....

Here are some ideas to begin with:

Character: Is your ideal partner quiet and thoughtful, or outgoing and chatty? Is this person hard-working and ambitious, or easy-going and happy with a job that simply pays the bills. You'll have grasped the idea - now carry on from here.

Qualities: Which qualities do you value in another person and why do they matter to you? Do they include honesty, loyalty, courage, determination and humour?

Looks: Is he tall or short; blond, red-haired or dark; fat or thin; blue-, brown- or green-eyed? Include any physical characteristics that you find attractive and sexy.

Habits: What habits do you like and which ones drive you crazy? Do you want someone who leaves clothes strewn around the house? Or a tidiness fanatic? This is your chance to come clean!

Beliefs: Do you want someone who believes in being faithful? In working through problems? In talking over his worries? Do you want someone with spiritual beliefs? Think of the beliefs you'd want a partner to share with you.

Skills and Talents: Do you want a great cook? A do-it-yourself expert? A scuba diver? Someone who speaks six languages or loves rock climbing?

Family and Friends: Is your ideal partner close to his family? Does he see them often? Does this person have lots of friends or just a few special ones? How will you fit in with the other people in your partner's life?

Hopes and Dreams: In some crucial areas, your partner's hopes and dreams need to match yours. Do you both want children? Do you want to live in the city or the country? Are you both ambitious or would you rather only one of you were?

When you've finished, mark the three most important items under each heading. These will form the basis of your mental checklist, the one you'll carry with you whenever you're meeting potential partners.

Know what you want
and you will be
certain to find it.

STEP FOURTEEN: WHAT CAN YOU OFFER?

Now you have reached the point where it is necessary to take a long, hard look at yourself and what you've got to offer in order to make your relationship really great. You're sure about what you want in a partner. You've thought hard about the vital qualities that will attract you and that you will value. But what will your future partner be attracted to in you and value most? What will make this person feel you're very special, and that he can trust and respect you?

To build a truly successful relationship, it's important that you share your basic values and beliefs, and that you live by the same code. In other words, if you want someone who's going to be faithful, honest, open and committed, you've got to be those things, too.

Of course, there will be differences between you, things that you love in each other and that you don't share. For instance, your partner may be very laid back, while you're more of a perfectionist. He may love being outdoors, while you'd rather curl up indoors with a good book. This kind of difference is fine, as long as it's something on which you can compromise. But there's no way to compromise on loyalty, honesty and commitment.

EXERCISE

Look at the qualities you put on your shopping list for your ideal partner (see pages 158-159). How many of those same qualities do you believe you possess yourself? How many have you shown in your previous relationships or in your life in general?

For instance, if you decided that you want someone faithful, understanding, open about their feelings and willing to share themselves and their lives, are you willing to behave in the same way?

Set about cultivating in yourself the qualities you want in someone else. Think hard about what they mean and what they entail. Being open about your feelings, for example, can be painful and difficult at times. If this is important to you, practise it whenever an opportunity comes along.

Also consider the qualities you do have and think of ones you need to develop or learn. Keep a mental list of the qualities you value most and check with yourself regularly to see whether you're practising them. Keep going until they become a part of you, as deeply ingrained as any habit you have without needing to think about it. Promise yourself that you will demonstrate, every single day, all the qualities that you admire and want to have - starting today.

> *When it comes to personal qualities, like will attract like.*

STEP FIFTEEN: BE FABULOUSLY ATTRACTIVE

Today you're going to have fun. This is the day when you become fabulously attractive and begin to attract other people to you like moths to a flame.

Becoming fabulously attractive has nothing at all to do with your looks. Of course, some people are naturally pretty or even beautiful, but even these people don't always attract others to them. In fact, many great beauties come across as quite cold and distant. Being fabulously attractive is a quality that anyone can have. It comes from deep inside and simply shines out of the people who have it.

We all know one or two people who are like this. People who light up a room, who are always surrounded by others and who are invited to everything because they're confident and fun to be with. People who are often described as beautiful but who, when you look closely, may not be conventionally beautiful at all.

These people have charisma by the truckload. And charisma - the ability to attract others effortlessly - is something you can cultivate and learn in a very short space of time.

How to be fabulously attractive:

Always look after yourself. Personal grooming is important. Take the trouble to exercise and eat healthily. Doing these things is a way of cherishing yourself. And when you cherish yourself, you feel good about yourself.

Always wear something you feel good in - throw out anything that doesn't make you feel you look great. If you go out wearing clothes you don't like, you can't feel attractive.

Talk to yourself as though you are the most attractive person you know. Tell yourself that you look stunning, compliment yourself often and give yourself a smile every time you pass a mirror.

Smile, often, when you're with other people. Practise smiling warmly at strangers - you'll be surprised how often they smile back. A smile equals instant attraction.

Relax. Nothing is more off-putting than a tense, stressed, anxious person. Someone who's relaxed, who behaves as though life is easy and fun, is attractive.

Imagine a deep well of beauty inside you, at the very core of who you are, and picture it spreading through you, then flowing out to the rest of the world. It is an intrinsic part of you, going with you wherever you go and making you fabulously attractive to anyone you meet.

Practise confidence, the most attractive quality of all. Truly confident people are comfortable with themselves, they handle power easily, they feel no need to impress or show off, they laugh at their mistakes while learning from them, they respect and value others and they feel good about who they are.

Think of people or public figures you admire who are self-assured and present well, and learn from them.

From today you are truly fabulously attractive.

STEP SIXTEEN: SPOIL YOURSELF

It is time to spoil yourself and make yourself feel truly special and wonderful. You're already taking the steps to feel attractive. Well, spoiling yourself is the next step. You deserve to feel wonderful about yourself, all the time. To feel wonderful you need to be pampered, nurtured and utterly spoiled. Who better to do this than you, as you know exactly what will make you feel fantastic?

This step is an important part of finding a lasting, fulfilling relationship. It is important not only because it will help you to feel good about yourself, but also because in a great relationship lovers love to spoil each other, to make each other feel great and to give each other treats. If you're going to find someone who will do this for you, you need to know exactly what it is that you would like him to do.

It is a universal truth that what you focus on grows. Whatever you are thinking about, believing in and putting your energy into is what you will get. So spoiling yourself, finding out which treats you most love and want from a partner, is where you need to put your focus right now.

Are you thinking that you never meet anyone who wants to spoil you and make you feel loved and gorgeous? Are you imagining that you never will? Stop right now! Believe it or not, most men are more than happy to spoil the women they love and to give them whatever makes them feel good. They just need to know what that is and to feel loved themselves in order to be loving.

Be loving towards yourself now and you'll find it easier to be loving towards your partner when you get together. Offer yourself fun, tenderness and pampering, and you'll be able to offer them to him, too. He will love this and return the attention to you. Here's what I want you to do:

Choose five things that make you feel absolutely wonderful and do them all today.

EXERCISE

Write a list of your new dating rules. Choose rules that you feel good about and know you'll be able to stick to. Here are some basic guidelines:

Alcohol: It's never a good idea to get drunk or to be out of control. How many drinks can you have before you need to stop? Know your limit, stick to it and don't let anyone pressure you in to drinking more.

Sex: It's always wise to wait until you know someone before having sex with them. Once you've had sex with someone, you feel under pressure (from yourself) to embark on a relationship. When you dig a little deeper, however, you may find that you don't even like the person. So give yourself at least a month or ten dates before deciding to have sex.

Money: Paying your share is a sensible approach. This doesn't necessarily mean splitting the bill in half every time you go out. It may be that you buy the drinks and the other person buys the meal. Paying your share is important, as it makes it easier for you to make decisions and take responsibility for what you do and what happens.

....

....

....

....

....

....

....

Once you've set your dating rules, learn them by heart and make a promise to yourself to stick to them. You'll enjoy yourself more, feel better about yourself and be able to let anyone you date know just how you like to do things.

Clever girls have
dating rules.

STEP EIGHTEEN: MEETING PEOPLE

Having identified the kind of person you want to meet, you now need to decide how you want to meet them. So many people wait to meet someone wonderful without thinking about where or how this is likely to happen.

They imagine they'll just bump into a future partner at the bus stop, sit next to them on the train or start chatting in the supermarket queue. Well, these things do happen from time to time, and maybe you will meet the person with whom you'll spend your life this way. But probably not, so putting in a little effort is well worthwhile.

Think about what kind of person you are and what you like doing. If you love clubbing, big crowds, loud music and dancing, you probably won't want to meet someone whose idea of heaven is a quiet night at home. Equally, if you love staying in, watching television, romantic dinners for two and intimate conversation, there's not much point in getting together with someone keen on partying every night. You need to meet someone whose social style is pretty similar to your own, otherwise you may end up never seeing each other! So identifying your style is the first step.

If you love going out to places where there are lots of people, it's going to be fairly easy to meet new people. But the drawback of big, noisy places is that it can be difficult to talk and strangers can jump into relationships without getting to know each other properly first. On the other hand, if you're the stay-at-home type, it's difficult to meet new people at all.

Work is an important factor here. Do you have a job in which you often meet new people and there are plenty of possible partners around? Lots of people meet their partners at work, so the right kind of job can offer good opportunities. But even if you work alone, with women only or in a tiny firm, don't worry because there are plenty of other ways to meet prospective partners.

Here are some possible ways:

* At parties.

* In pubs and wine bars.

* Through sports and health clubs.

* Through activities - anything from dancing classes to wine-tasting.

* Through online dating websites.

Think about the ways in which you'd like to meet someone and how these fit with your lifestyle and social style. Are you willing to make changes, free up more time, put in the effort? If so, it's time for the most vital step of all - taking action.

Every new person you meet draws you a step closer to meeting the love of your life.

STEP NINETEEN: TAKE ACTION

Now is the time to take action! You've got the self-belief, you know who and what you want and you know, without a doubt, that you can bring whatever you want into your life. That's why it's time to go for it!

Action is the key to change: it's the key to having what you want in life and without it even the best beliefs in the world won't carry you far. Action means following up your words and beliefs with deeds, it means doing whatever you need to and proving to yourself that you are serious about what you want.

Action takes courage, willpower and trust. You need courage to do things differently, to stick your neck out and take a risk, and to cope with change. You need willpower to see your actions through, no matter how scary that is, and to hang in there through the tough times. You need trust because it means that you know, with absolute certainty, that what you want and deserve will come to you if you go for it.

So what action do you need to take today?

Here are some of the possibilities:

* Sign up for online dating, or download a dating app.

* Organize a party and ask guests to bring a single person they know.

* Chat up someone you like the look of.

* Invite someone you find attractive out on a date.

* Sign up for an evening class that interests you.

* Tell friends that you'd like to meet new people and ask them for introductions.

* Join the gym.

* Arrange a night out with a couple of friends at a wine bar or pub in an interesting part of town.

You get the idea! Why not do all of these things, then try some more of your own as well. The point is to put lots of energy into doing whatever may lead to meeting someone wonderful. Don't stop at one or two things: be brave, be bold and give yourself plenty of options.

Of course, it doesn't make sense to do anything you won't enjoy. Pick things that will give you a buzz, be fun, teach you something new, get you fit or improve your social life. You can have a great time on the way to fulfilling your goal.

When you take action, you reap rewards.

STEP TWENTY: ASK FOR WHAT YOU WANT

Crunch time. I want you to be prepared to ask, loud and clear, for what you want. And when it comes to finding a partner, one of the best ways is online. There are plenty of good dating websites, both free and paid. In fact these days two out of five single people between the age of 20 and 50 have used internet dating sites and 40 million people around the world are looking for love online.

If your first response is, "I'm not that desperate", think again. Countless well-adjusted, interesting, clever, good-looking and fun people look for commitment online.

Why? Because it's easy and convenient, it opens up your choices and it gives you a chance to meet people you'd never normally meet and to choose exactly who you want to date and who you don't. So take the plunge and give it a try. Asking for what you want, with courage and conviction, will leave you glowing with confidence.

HERE ARE SOME TIPS:

Do some research first and pick a site that feels right for you. You may prefer a general site, or one that caters for a group you feel part of. There are sites for everyone - including single parents, divorcees, professionals and students.

Take a bit of trouble over your profile and picture. Try to give a good idea of what you're interested in, what you're looking for and what's important to you.

Be honest. If you want a loving partner who's not afraid of commitment, say so. A lot of people want the same. If you sound too jokey, you'll attract people who'll waste your time.

Reject anyone who sounds much too old or young, or says

something in their message which you don't like or which doesn't fit with who you are and what you want.

Give people a chance if they sound shy, nervous or a bit serious. You can always find out more over the phone, or even meet for an hour.

When you go on a date be generous at the beginning. People can seem strained and awkward in this kind of situation but be very different once they're at ease.

At the very least joining a dating site will add to your choice of partners. And that's the idea - to meet a variety of people, as eventually one of them will be the person you'll fall in love with.

Ask for what you want and you will get it.

STEP TWENTY-ONE: PREPARING TO DATE

If you've followed the plan so far, very soon you'll be going on dates - lots of them. Think of this as the chance to have heaps of fun, meet new people, go to exciting places and enjoy yourself. Don't be tempted to bypass the dating stage and plunge straight into a relationship, even if you think you've met your ideal partner. The odds are that the first, second or third date won't be THE one. So be prepared to meet lots of people - and give yourself lots of choice.

Dating is an essential preliminary stage before you settle into a relationship. It's a chance to have a good time while fine-tuning your ability to distinguish relationship potential from relationship no-nos. If dating is going to be a big success, you need to prepare. So today's task is to make sure you're absolutely ready for dating to begin.

YOUR PRE-DATING CHECKLIST

1 Line up petcare or childcare if you need it. Make sure you have someone reliable to call on at short notice. "I can't get a babysitter" is a deadly dull dating excuse. "I can't leave my cat on his own" is worse.

Line up a friend, too - not to go with you (that's tacky and a recipe for disaster), but to know where you are and who you're with if you go on any blind dates.

2 Clear your diary. This is especially important if you're a workaholic. It's time to put yourself and your love life first. Make sure you've got several days a week free for dates. When potential dates come along, you don't want to be booking them for a month ahead - you could seem overbusy, wary or unenthusiastic, and no one will wait around long enough to find out how wonderful you really are.

3 Think of interesting venues that you'd be comfortable going to with new dates. If you're the one who suggests where you meet, it gives you an instant advantage and makes you sound like someone who goes out a lot, whether you actually do or not. Suggest places that are easy to get to, fun to be in, attractive and popular, but not so busy or loud that you can't get comfortable or hear yourself speak. When you are on a date, you want to be able to sit, talk, stop talking without a deadly silence descending, and get home easily.

If you don't know any suitable places, ask friends, look around your area, check out places you pass by and generally do some research.

4 Sort out your wardrobe. Dating crisis number one is: "I don't know what to wear." Avoid it by working out what you feel great in right now. Go and look through your clothes. If there's nothing you think is suitable for the occasion, it's time to go shopping. If there's something you feel comfortable and at ease in, yet still sexy and attractive, great - keep it ready.

Checklist completed?

You're ready to
begin dating!

STEP TWENTY-TWO: DATING

So you've cleared the way, lined up the dates, sorted out your wardrobe and you're all set to go. Fantastic. Today it's time to think about how you want your dates to go and what will make you feel relaxed and confident when dating someone you don't know well - or at all!

First of all remember what a date is - and isn't:

It is: An opportunity to get to know someone, to decide whether you'd like to see him again, to let someone get to know you, to share drinks and food and conversation, and to forget about the routine things in life and enjoy yourself.

It's not: A lifetime's contract, a promise to have sex, a bargaining forum (food for sex), a chore, an ordeal, a meeting of souls or the chance for a few free drinks.

The most important thing you can do on a date is to treat the person you're with as a human being. Remember that they're probably nervous and likely to have made an effort. They also want it to work out and may be trying a bit too hard to impress you. So give them a chance.

If you don't know what to talk about, ask your date questions about their life, interests and family. Almost everyone loves to talk about themselves. If they won't talk, or are evasive and vague, take it as a possible warning sign, as it may mean that they keep secrets, are holding back or are going to be hard work.

Other warning signs to watch out for include:

* They talk about themselves nonstop.

* They boast a lot.

* They have no sense of humour.

Warning signs mean you should think twice about a second date, although don't rule it out if a warning sign is counterbalanced by something you really like about them (apart from looks). But be aware that warning signs often indicate traits that would be difficult to put up with in the long run. It may be better to say no now, rather than later.

Remember, a date that doesn't work out simply leaves an opening for a date with someone else. A date that does work out and leads to another date is exciting enough to be worth all the effort and all the nerves.

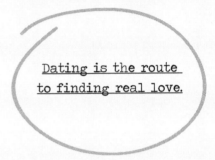

Dating is the route to finding real love.

STEP TWENTY-THREE: BEWARE OF THUNDERBOLTS

The more people you meet, the more dates you can go on. Of course, you may meet the right person straight away. It is more likely, however, that you will have to go out with a few people before you find the one who is right for you.

Some of the people you date may seem wrong from the outset. Still, think about why they seem wrong before you decide against a second date. If the reason is something that gets on your nerves and is unlikely to change, such as arrogance, sarcasm or self-obsession, then fine, don't go back there! If you like the person, however, but don't feel any particular chemistry, be willing to see him again and let the liking deepen. You may be surprised by what happens.

In these days of fast pace and fast living, we have come to expect that everything will happen fast. If instant attraction isn't there, we dismiss someone. In most strong, happy relationships, though, love and attraction have grown, inch by inch.

In fact the people we feel instantly attracted to can often be the ones to avoid. If you have a history of falling for men at once, only to be disappointed, don't let yourself do it again. Instant attraction is fun - the buzz is exciting, the promise enormous. But then, pretty soon afterwards, so is the disappointment. That's why today I want you to beware of thunderbolts. When mutual attraction hits us like a thunderbolt, it's often disastrous.

Why? Because when that happens it's not the person to whom we are attracted. How can it be? We don't really know them. It's simply that this person has triggered something in us, a recognition, usually connected to the past.

For instance, suppose Jane's father was a charming, irresponsible man who could never commit or stay in a relationship and who wasn't around much when Jane was young. As his child, however, she loved him and thought he was perfect. Even when she grew up and knew he wasn't perfect, she still loved him and longed for his interest and attention.

When she started having relationships with men, she chose partners just like her father. Of course, she never thought they'd be like him - some of them seemed very different at first. But there was always an instant attraction and Jane didn't wait to find out what they were really like before getting involved. The same pattern always re-emerged eventually: her partners, just like her father, left her.

If you find yourself attracted to someone immediately, then go very, very slowly. Promise yourself lots of time to get to know this person. Stand back a little, put the attraction aside and think about what he is really like. It may be that you need to bypass this kind of attraction in order to find the person who is right for you. Attraction that has grown more slowly generally lasts much longer.

The bigger the thunderbolt, the more likely the disaster.

STEP TWENTY-FOUR: GO FOR GOLD

Remember that nothing but the best will do for you. Finding love is not about settling for anyone who comes along, or even for someone who seems halfway right. It's about finding someone who is worthy of the love you have to give, and that means someone who is really special in every way - pure gold. That's why I want you to go for gold and to make this your motto in your search for love.

It's easy to come across people who are the equivalent of fool's gold. In other words, they appear to be wonderful, until you look a little deeper. That's why it's so crucial to take your time in getting to know someone and to find out what kind of person they really are. Surface glitz is attractive and charm is magnetic, but lasting relationships need more than these. Be aware that people who make a dazzling first impression can prove very different in the long term.

Women are often attracted to the kind of men who treat them badly, who don't call, who let them down, ignore them, criticize them or hurt them. So many women say: "I don't know why I always go for mean men."

Well, here are some reasons:

* Mean men can seem exciting at first.

* They seem more of a challenge.

* Women who like mean men believe, deep down, that they don't deserve anyone better and that the choice is a mean man or no one at all.

The same women often justify their choice by saying that nice men are boring. Of course, there are pleasant men who are also bland and dull. Men who are honest, open, not afraid of commitment, generous and loving, however, are not boring. They're fantastic! They make better lovers, better partners and better friends than the mean sort ever will. They're the kind of man you need to look for if you want a good, long-term relationship.

Who would choose suffering over being loved and made to feel cherished? Only a woman who doesn't know her own worth.

If you believe that you're pure gold and that anyone would be lucky to be with you, you'll go for someone who's pure gold. And that means someone worthy of you.

Go for gold - you deserve the best.

STEP TWENTY-FIVE: IGNORE SETBACKS

Now it's time to look at the way you deal with problems and setbacks. In finding the right relationship for you, there will inevitably be the occasional hiccup. Things go wrong from time to time - that's part of life. The important thing is how you deal with them. You can take them to heart, worry, agonize and feel depressed about it. Or you can feel temporarily disappointed, then carry right on with your plan.

What can go wrong? Here are some possible examples:

* You are stood up on a date.

* You really like someone, but they don't want to see you again.

* They say they'll call, but don't.

* You think you've found the one, rush into a relationship and then get dumped - they only wanted a fling.

* You've met one or two nice people, but they don't ask you out.

* You just can't find the courage to go on a blind date.

* You made a complete fool of yourself by doing something that embarrassed both you and your date.

There are plenty of other possible hiccups. I'm sure you can come up with a few!

So what should you do when something like this happens? Here's what:

* Give yourself up to an hour to feel really disappointed, annoyed, idiotic or hurt.

* After the hour is up, THAT'S IT. Simply refuse to dwell on it or to indulge those unhappy feelings any more.

* Remind yourself that if he behaved badly he's not worth a second of your time or a moment of your energy and interest.

* Be glad that you found out sooner rather than later that he's not good enough for you.

* Arrange to see a good friend and LAUGH with her about what happened. Don't tell it like a sad story, but as a funny one. Don't spend too long on it - ten minutes is enough, and refuse to analyse the situation. Instead, move on to talking about something else.

* Do something straight away to move you on your way towards your goal. Arrange another date, plan another party - whatever's next on the list.

This is how you prove that you can take disappointment lightly - it's a skill you'll need all your life. Okay, so you were let down or made an idiot of yourself. So what? So on to better things, that's what. Keep your disappointments small - don't let them grow by focusing on them.

Remember that every person in a successful relationship will have experienced disappointments along the way. Some of them will have had many. You can either give in or you can laugh in the face of disappointment and get back out there!

Take setbacks lightly and carry straight on.

STEP TWENTY-SIX: TAKE YOUR TIME

Today I want you to focus on the importance of taking your time and going slowly into a relationship. Why? Because there's a simple truth that applies to 99 per cent of relationships:

The faster you go in, the more likely it is to end quickly.

We tend to go into relationships at the same speed we come out of them. If you rush into a relationship, starry-eyed and convinced that because a man is gorgeous he's perfect for you and longing to commit, you lose your sense of balance. Speed, like drink, impairs the judgment. And the further in you get, the more you feel you have to make it work, even if you discover something you don't like or trust about him.

On the other hand, progressing slowly - getting to know someone, dating, holding hands, holding back until you feel more certain - has everything going for it. You never lose your sense of judgment, so you can see, far more clearly, what this person is really like.

By taking your time you may learn things that may make you think twice about going deeper into a relationship with him. For instance, he might be an alcoholic, he might be a serial womanizer, he might be hung up on his ex and not emotionally free, he might be about to be fired, he might be too attached to his parents, he might not have any friends or he might be unreliable and irresponsible. All these are things you can only find out over time, as they're not the sort of things you could detect about most people on a first or second date.

When you rush in, you get all of the fun part over with very fast. The buzz, the heat, the first touch, the first kiss and so on . . . You can have more fun when you take the relationship slowly. Spin it out and add anticipation to the joy of being around someone who attracts and excites you.

Ending it is easier when you go slowly. When you haven't dived in deep, it's much easier to walk away if something begins to feel wrong. This is important, as the more time you spend with someone who isn't right, the longer you put off being with someone who is.

If you find yourself tempted to rush in fast (and almost everyone has rushed in, at some point), slow yourself down by:

* Letting a week pass before you go on another date.

* Reading this step to yourself again.

* Reminding yourself that, if he's worth knowing, he'll be glad that you want to get to know the real him.

* Making an agreement with a friend that you won't get deeply involved in less than six weeks, and report back regularly.

* Telling him at the outset that you don't want to rush into anything - he'll be intrigued.

Take your time and reap the rewards.

STEP TWENTY-SEVEN: STAY OPEN

It's time to remind yourself to stay open to all the possibilities that dating and meeting new men can bring. This means being aware of danger signs as well as being aware of potential. It means being choosy, but not too choosy.

In other words, while you're dating, use your intuition and judgment to decide who might be worth getting to know a little more and who is a definite no-no. Here are some examples to guide you:

DANGER SIGNS

He drinks heavily or he takes drugs
Remember that it's impossible to get to know someone who's drunk or taking drugs. Alcohol and drugs mask feelings and alter behaviour.

He has no money
This could be a regular state for him, and you might end up poorer because of it.

He never stops joking
Men with this tendency are often insecure and trying to cover up that insecurity. The flip side of a joker can be someone who is dark and depressing.

He has lots of mates or acquaintances, but no real friends
Someone like this finds genuine relationships difficult. He prefers to keep things at a superficial level, an attribute you may later grow to hate.

He shows off
Boasting is boring and another sign of insecurity.

He takes no real interest in you
If he finds you attractive, but can't be bothered to ask about you or remember things you've told him about yourself, he considers this a short-term affair.

He's thoughtless towards you
He leaves you to follow him into places, leaves you nursing a drink while he chats to friends, assumes you don't want to eat if he doesn't - this kind of attitude tends to get worse with time, not better.

He has never found a job he likes
A lot of self-esteem, especially for men, is tied up with work. If he hates his job, he probably doesn't feel good about himself.

ENCOURAGING SIGNS:

* He is genuinely interested in what you have to say.

* He likes his job (or he's changing it).

* He confides in you about what he feels, thinks and dreams of.

* He treats you well and makes you feel good.

* He talks warmly about his close friends.

* He can, at times, be very funny.

* He is generous with his money.

* He's solvent (that is, he meets his financial responsibilities).

* He knows why his past relationships went wrong and he doesn't just blame ex-partners.

Nothing's written in stone. A danger sign doesn't necessarily rule a man out: it only suggests that you need to be very careful and keep your eyes open. Equally, a couple of encouraging signs doesn't mean he's right for you in every way.

Stay open to the possibilities and trust yourself.

STEP TWENTY-EIGHT: STAY ON TRACK

Today's the day to remind yourself to stay on track and keep going, however much effort this requires.

Finding love means being prepared for hard work. It's not enough to love the idea of falling in love. To find real love you need dedication, determination and courage. You need to be willing to take risks, say no when you have to, say yes even when it's scary and hang on in there even when you feel like giving up. And there are bound to be moments when you feel like giving up, when it would be a lot easier to curl up in front of the television with a box of chocolates and think: "Oh well, I gave it a shot and it didn't work." But you want to find love, not settle for excuses, so when you reach that point you're going to finish the chocolates, get up out of your cosy armchair and keep on going.

EXERCISE

Pick a quiet time to try this keep-going strategy. Make sure there won't be any interruptions, and lie or sit somewhere comfortable with your eyes closed:

Imagine that somewhere out there is a man who is going to make you incredibly happy. A man who understands you, who is strong and caring, who'll hang on in there even on the days when you feel like pushing him away. This man has humour, generosity, compassion and depth. He has energy, he's intelligent, he's interesting and he knows how to work hard. He's also incredibly sexy.

Of course, he's human, he has faults. So have you. There will be days when he irritates you or gets it wrong. On balance, however, the good outweighs the bad by ten to one and you will love him and be loved by him enough to get through absolutely anything together.

On a certain day, which is already in the universal diary, you're going to meet this man. As long as you don't let it pass you by. If you're sitting at home doing nothing, wasting your time with a loser or giving up on love, the day and the man will carry on past you. But if you put your energy, motivation and attention towards this meeting, it will happen, and the day may come much sooner than you think.

You deserve him. You deserve the best. You deserve happiness. So go for it.

Staying on track means being willing to take the next step, even when you really don't want to. It means keeping your goal clearly in mind and knowing that the goal is more important than anything that happens along the way. It means believing, with all your heart, that you will achieve your goal.

If you feel you're sliding off the track, say to yourself:

* I know I can do this.

* I never give up on something I've set out to do.

* I deserve a great person to love and I'm going to find him.

* I've got courage and willpower.

* Every minute of every day I'm getting closer to the love I want.

<u>Stay on track
towards the love
you deserve.</u>

STEP TWENTY-NINE: REVIEW YOUR PROGRESS

Take a good look at exactly what you've done and achieved so far and decide whether you need to add or change anything.

First of all, go back through the previous 28 steps and assess how you've done. Did you skip any? Skim over a few? Feel half-hearted about one or two? It's useful to look at this, as the chances are that the ones you most resisted are the ones you most need to do. That's the way life often works. We protest, reassure ourselves and make excuses, but in the end it's usually the things we do our utmost to avoid that we most need to face.

It's worth being honest with yourself and then going back and doing the step or steps that you missed. Being half-hearted won't find you love. Facing up to the things you don't want to deal with will. Whatever you missed will be a vital key in your progress towards love. So don't short-change yourself: give yourself 100 per cent backing by doing every step fully.

In the same way, if there was a step that felt especially good to you and seemed to strike a deep chord, go over it again. Many of the steps will have carried through with you throughout the following days and will have created new beliefs and behaviours that will remain with you.

Once you've reviewed the steps up to this point, look at the action you've taken to meet new men and make dates. Have you been taking action, day in, day out, to do this? If so, how is it going? Are you flagging a little or feeling love is as far away as ever? Or are you full of energy and excitement, and raring to go? If so, great. If you're flagging, however, go back over the early steps in the book to reboost your self-belief and motivation.

Remember that success is a combination of belief and consistent action. A burst of energy that fizzles out won't do it. You need to keep taking action, every day, until you eventually reach your goal. Now is a good time to create an action plan to work with over the coming weeks.

EXERCISE

Think about the steps you can take, day by day, to move you closer to love. The calls you need to make, the people you need to talk to, the places you need to go to, the self-belief you need to reinforce.

Write out an action plan and keep it in your handbag or somewhere close to you and look at it often. Change it when you need to - the best plans are flexible and can be adapted. Add fresh ideas to your action plan whenever you can and update it whenever you achieve a success.

Make progress every day towards finding love.

STEP THIRTY: CELEBRATE!

You've made it through to the end of the 30 steps and now you deserve to celebrate. Celebrating is a way of saying to yourself "Well done" and of appreciating yourself and your efforts.

Celebrating means hanging out, having fun, feeling good and letting everyone else join in, so it's a good idea to do it often! Here's what you've got to celebrate:

* Your determination.

* Your courage.

* Your willingness to keep going.

* Your ability to have fun.

* Your adventurousness.

* Your humour.

* The steps that you've taken towards finding love.

* The fact that you've found love or that you're about to do so.

* The fact that you've discovered what an AMAZING human being you are.

* All the successes you've already had, no matter how big or small.

How to celebrate? Think about what you most enjoy doing and use it as a way of celebrating. You could:

* Throw a party.

* Invite a few friends over.

* Go out for a meal.

* Buy yourself a bottle of champagne.

* Give yourself a present.

* Dance to music you love.

* Fill your home with flowers.

* Make eye contact with a gorgeous stranger on the way to work.

* Wear an outfit in which you feel sexy.

Or you could do all of them!

Whatever you do, do it for pure pleasure, with energy and love. Remember that celebrating is a big part of finding love, and that, when you're with the right person, celebrating happens easily and often. So get in practice, know how you love to celebrate and enjoy every moment.

Celebrate the joy of finding real love.

A FINAL WORD

Following the steps in this book will have set you on your path towards finding the love you want and deserve. It has given you a blueprint you can continue to work from until you've found that lasting and rewarding love. Even then, it's important that you keep your new beliefs, attitudes and energy, as they'll carry you on to a successful future, building and sustaining your loving relationship.

Never let doubts about reaching your goal get the better of you. Having doubts is just the same as feeling scared. Feeling scared is fine, as long as you carry on anyway. If you stop when you're scared, you are giving in to the belief that what you fear is true.

Remember that what you concentrate on grows, so focus on the positive, the exciting, the wonderful, the joyful and the adventurous. Keep your beliefs strong and clear, and know, in your heart and mind and soul, that love is your right.

RELATIONSHIPS

Being in a relationship with someone you love is a truly wonderful thing. It's exciting, rewarding, enlightening and inspiring, but also hard work, challenging, painful and scary. Will it last? Can you really share your life, now and for ever, with this one person? Who doesn't ask herself those questions, no matter how good the relationship is? And when you are going through a rough patch, you may ask them about a hundred times a day.

Society sells us the fantasy that love will be a totally wondrous experience. We don't like to hear that love will involve pain as well as pleasure - that's what we learn as we go along. Sticking with a relationship, being committed and making it work are huge achievements. Courage is needed to hang on in there when the going gets tough, to learn from your mistakes and to carry on even when you're hurting. But it is more than worth it. To be in a loving relationship is to be blessed; it will bring deep happiness, benefit your health and enrich your life.

Follow this 30-step plan, and you will get the support and encouragement you need, tools for change, and greater resources and understanding to help you keep the love you've found and make the relationship the best it can be.

"LOVING SOMEONE SHOULD NOT MEAN LOSING YOU. LOVE EMPOWERS YOU. IT SHOULDN'T ERASE YOU."

THEMA DAVIS

STEP ONE: REAL LOVE

So you've found someone to love. Fabulous! Whether it's been six days, six weeks, six years or longer, you want to make it work and for this relationship to be the one that lasts and grows stronger and better every day. That's why today, at the very beginning of this challenge, you need to take a look at what love is and what it means to you. Love is discussed constantly and much has been written about it. But what is it? We may see images of hearts and flowers, talk of romance and excitement, joy and passion, but although love can include all these things, they don't explain what it is.

Some things love isn't:

* Chasing after someone who doesn't really want you.

* Letting yourself be smothered, hurt or put down.

* Trying to mould yourself into something you think you should be.

* Always going along with what your partner wants.

* Bouncing continually between highs and lows, excitement and tears.

* Presenting only the "acceptable" part of yourself to someone.

* Drama, gossip, pretence or flattery.

* Staying with someone to avoid being alone.

* Shunning real closeness and intimacy.

* Trying to fix someone or have them fix you.

If you are doing any of the above, it's time to stop and review the relationship. This doesn't mean the relationship has to end, but you may need to try to do some things differently and see whether the relationship is strong enough to survive the changes.

Some things love is:

* Letting your partner know the real you, warts and all.

* Taking the time and trouble to get to know him, warts and all.

* Growing and learning together.

* Respecting one another.

* Developing trust between you.

* Staying committed even when you want to run away.

* Liking your partner.

* Sharing fears, doubts, hopes and dreams.

* Taking responsibility for yourself.

* Accepting what you don't like in your partner as well as what you do.

Think about the relationship. How many of the above are true for you and your partner? What strengths and weaknesses does the relationship have? Are there changes you need to make in yourself? What would you like to change about the way the two of you are together?

You may find that you are very clear on these points, which is a strong asset - you're already a step ahead. However, if you suspect things aren't quite right, but aren't sure why, don't worry; you will become clearer about any existing problems and what needs to be done about them as you work through the 30-step plan. Think of this day as the first step on an adventure, because that is what a relationship is - an adventure for two.

Be wise about love and choose the path to real love.

STEP TWO: DREAMS

Look at the dreams you have for your relationship. We all have dreams, hopes and wishes that are precious and that we often keep secret from anyone else, fantasies of how things might be and of what we would love to happen. These dreams are important - we all need to believe that wonderful things are possible. And wonderful things can and do happen, but not without effort from us. We each need to make our own dreams come true.

Every relationship needs dreams because they create goals and give you and your partner a path to follow. Your dreams may be romantic, sensual, passionate and exciting. They may involve a big white wedding, setting up home in a country cottage with a picket fence, sailing around the world or raising a brood of children. Alternatively, your dreams may be more practical. Perhaps you imagine giving up your job, working with your partner to create your own business together or supporting your partner so that he can follow a dream of his own.

Take a long, hard look at your dreams. Do they focus around changes in your partner or in yourself? Do you dream that your partner will be kinder, more loving or more available? Do you dream of a time when you stop arguing or hurting each other?

EXERCISE

Write down the dreams you have for your relationship. Imagine it is a year from now and then five years from now. What is the relationship like? What are you both doing, where do you live and how do you get along? Keep this as a record, adding to it as new wishes, hopes and dreams occur to you.

....

....

....

....

....

Over the next four weeks, begin making your dreams more possible and real. To do this, break them down into small steps and begin taking those steps, one by one. Even if your dreams seem a long way off or impossible, you can begin moving towards them. What would you need to do to make your dreams come true? What steps could you take, right now, to begin?

First, tell your partner about your dreams. Sharing is a little scary because it makes us feel vulnerable, but it is exciting, too, because it makes our dreams become more real. Telling your partner will give him important information about you. Ask him to tell you about his dreams. Do you dream of the same things? Even if you don't, you can help and encourage one another so that some of your dreams do come true.

Think about other steps you can take. Do you need to open up more, to be braver about asking for what you want, to be firmer about saying no, or to work fewer hours, change jobs or start saving? Take the first step right now, and bring your dreams out of the shadows and into the open.

Make your dreams come true and keep love alive.

STEP THREE: GROWING CLOSER

What does it mean to be close? Think about how close you and your partner are and look at ways of growing even closer. Intimacy is the basis of a good relationship, and it means being able to be open and to reveal your innermost thoughts to your partner without fear of being laughed at, criticized or rejected. To be really emotionally close to another person is wonderful because you can be yourself with them - no pretence, no effort, no cover-up - just you, as you are. To feel that you are loved and accepted for yourself means that you can relax, that you can make mistakes safe in the knowledge that they won't make any difference to the way you are loved.

We all have a "shop front" that we present to the world, the part of us we think is attractive and acceptable. Then we have the "back room', the stuff we keep hidden at first because we're not so proud of it. In an intimate relationship you can't keepthe back room hidden, even if you try, and neither can your partner. Inevitably you are both going to show the sides of yourselves that you like the least - the aspects you fear will cause rejection or ridicule. When we are loved, instead of put down, we are fully accepted, and that's the best feeling in the world. But to be loved in this way you must be willing to let your partner know the real you.

How much have you let your partner know?

Tick yes to the following questions if they apply. Does your partner know:

☐ Your deepest fears and insecurities.

☐ The biggest hurts you've suffered in the past.

☐ The worst thing that's ever happened to you.

☐ What you are most ashamed of in your life.

☐ Who you love and who you hate.

☐ Your biggest embarrassment.

☐ How you really feel about your body.

☐ What you look like without any make-up in an old pair of pyjamas.

☐ The changes you would like to make to yourself.

☐ What you think your weaknesses and failings are.

How many times did you answer yes? This number will give you a clue about how intimate you are with your partner. If you answered yes fewer than seven times, you could allow your partner to come closer. Now ask yourself whether you know the answer to all these questions about your partner. How close does he let you come?

Make a decision today to allow your partner to come closer to the real you. To do this, simply be willing to open up and let him know more about you - the no-frills you. Offer information, talk about yourself and ask in return. Remember what your partner tells you and treat the information with respect. Let the relationship be a mutual journey of discovery.

Show the real you and grow closer every day.

STEP FOUR: BE HONEST

Let's look at honesty today, because if you want your partner to be honest then you must be honest, too. There are many ways of being dishonest in a relationship, including some which might not, at first, seem like dishonesty. But even subtle kinds attract problems and difficulties. Being honest can be hard at times and it can take a lot of courage, but the reward will be a healthy, strong relationship.

Ways in which we can be dishonest with our partner:

* You regularly flirt with someone else in a way you know would upset your partner; you tell yourself it's okay because your partner doesn't know about it.

* You fancy someone else and you've kissed; you tell yourself that you are not being unfaithful because you haven't had sex.

* You don't say what you really think in discussions with your partner.

* You don't express how you really feel about something important, such as sex, money or children.

* You lie about the past or about what you are up to now.

* You aren't straightforward about money matters.

Do you recognize any of the above? Are any true of you? Are there other ways in which, deep down, you know that you are not being truthful? If so, it's time to stop - today. When we are dishonest with others, it is impossible to feel really good about ourselves or to have a genuinely loving and happy relationship. Those things you have been untruthful about seem to grow bigger and more important as time goes on. You think of them more often and it can become exhausting. Invest in the relationship by telling the truth and behaving in an honest and open manner.

Being honest doesn't mean that you have to tell everything. If your partner is sensitive about past relationships, don't present a list of names and dates. There is always a place for discretion, and it is unnecessary to disclose something that will hurt your partner if it isn't relevant to the present. Honesty is about being authentic and truthful right now, about the issues that matter between you. It's about speaking up when it counts and trusting that you can find a way to sort out disagreements. It's about putting your partner and the relationship first, before anyone or anything else.

> Be honest with your partner and yourself, and feel great.

STEP FIVE: RESPECT YOURSELF

Respect may sound like an old-fashioned word, but in any good relationship it matters enormously. This task is to consider just how much you respect yourself. If you treat yourself with respect, you are far more likely to be treated with respect by your partner. Other people respond to the signals we give them, so if you don't think well of yourself, others will sense it and respond accordingly. So what exactly does respect mean? It means treating yourself in a caring, considerate and decent way. Knowing your standards, sticking to them and believing that your opinions, thoughts and feelings have value.

Behaviour where self-respect is missing. Do you recognize any of these?

☐ You let your partner steamroller your opinions or feelings.

☐ You put up with being physically abused by your partner.

☐ You permit your partner to flirt even though this hurts you.

☐ You suspect your partner is unfaithful, but avoid taking steps to find out.

☐ You allow your partner to make all the decisions.

☐ You let your partner speak to you in an insulting or degrading way.

☐ You speak in an insulting way, or shout and scream when upset.

☐ You allow your partner to be rude to you in front of friends.

☐ You don't look after yourself by eating well, sleeping enough, getting exercise and caring for your body.

☐ You put yourself down in conversation.

☐ You tell yourself that you can't expect faithfulness/consideration/kindness because you're not worth it.

There are many other examples of lack of self-respect, but we usually know instinctively when it is missing. Lack of self-respect is about low self-esteem; when self-esteem is low, standards drop. Standards are vital in a relationship. You need to know what you think is right in order to judge whether something measures up to it or not. If you are behaving with a lack of self-respect, decide today to raise your self-esteem and standards, and to respect yourself - you will feel so much better when you do.

How to boost self-respect:

* Never put up with any kind of bad treatment, such as violence, rudeness or unkindness. Make the message clear and, in extreme cases (especially violence), remove yourself from the situation until changes have occurred.

* Tell yourself that your feelings and opinions matter. Listen to them, trust them and follow them.

* Treat yourself in a loving, generous and considerate way.

* Make a list of standards you consider important, such as "Violence is unacceptable", "Being faithful is vital", and keep to them (see also Know Your Boundaries, page 234).

When you love and value yourself,
you help others to treat you
likewise, and you will find it
easier to walk away from anyone
who persists in treating you badly.

*Treat yourself with
respect and invite the
respect of others.*

STEP SIX: RESPECT YOUR PARTNER

Just as it is vital to respect yourself, it is also very important to
respect your partner. Love without mutual respect is sadly flawed.
Take today to examine whether your behaviour towards your partner is
respectful, considerate and kind.

In a long-term relationship, contempt can easily creep in. You may begin
to take your partner for granted, to stop noticing those attributes that
made you fall in love and to be aware only of the traits that irritate
or annoy you. In doing this, you are focusing on the negative. There
is a universal truth, which states, "What you focus on grows". When you
concentrate on what you don't like, on your frustration, irritation or
anxiety, it will grow. While focusing on the positive will increase the
positive potential in the relationship.

Examples of treating your partner without respect. Are any of the
following true of you?

☐ You make decisions without consultation.

☐ You plan your own life and expect him to fit in with it.

☐ You often criticize.

☐ You point out all the things he can't do.

☐ You put down or ridicule your partner in front of others.

☐ You forget anniversaries that are important to him.

☐ You are rude about your partner's family or friends.

☐ You are not interested in his feelings, wishes or needs.

☐ You are often impatient.

☐ You keep trying to make your partner change.

If even one is, you need to think about what is going on in the relationship. One partner is often stronger and more dominant than the other and may find it easy to lose respect for the partner who is slower, quieter, less dynamic, less confident or less outspoken. However, relationships need balance and most people need someone who is different from themselves in key ways. Learn to respect your partner for his qualities, talents and abilities. Perhaps he is slower and more reserved than you, but also more romantic and generous. Stop judging and believing that fast is better than slow, or that talking a lot is better than listening quietly.

EXERCISE

What are your partner's positive qualities? Remind yourself of the qualities that made you fall in love with him, then list them and start to notice them again. Recognize and write down the ways in which you balance one another.

Your partner deserves your best, not your worst. Many people treat strangers better than the person they love most. Imagine this scenario. A guest comes to dinner and spills a glass of wine on the carpet. What would you say? You would say it didn't matter, clear it up, bring another glass and try to make him or her feel at ease.

If your partner spilled the wine, would you do the same? Or would you explode?

Begin to focus on the positive in your partner and the relationship. Bite your tongue when you feel a criticism coming and choose to say something appreciative instead. Speak warmly and treat your partner with love and respect. Remember that you are both equally important, valuable and special.

Respect your partner and the relationship will flourish.

STEP SEVEN: WHAT ABOUT ARGUMENTS?

All couples argue: some often, some rarely, most from time to time. Disagreements aren't necessarily a bad thing; in fact, many very happy couples have the occasional ferocious row and feel it's not a problem.

Be honest about the kind of arguments you generally have. "Good" rows are underpinned by genuine liking and respect for one another. You can get issues off your chest but at the same time you both know where the boundaries lie. The row doesn't cause lasting hurt or carry on for hours. When one of you makes a "peace move" - a word, gesture or look that says: "Come on, let's stop" - the other responds by softening. Sometimes, however, arguments are a symptom of something wrong with the relationship.

When to worry about arguments:

* You end up simply swapping insults.

* The argument goes on for hours or even days.

* A serious row occurs every week or even more often.

* Hurtful things are said which you deeply regret.

* Language is cutting, cruel, critical or contemptuous.

* You ignore each other's attempts to defuse the argument.

* Walking away for half an hour doesn't cool you down.

* Violence, including slamming doors, throwing things and hitting or hurting yourself or the other person, is a feature of your arguments.

In a healthy argument, you may shout, argue and stomp around, but you do not get violent or blurt out things that you afterwards seriously regret. Criticism and contempt undermine any relationship; when these creep in, restoring goodwill, love and kindness becomes harder and harder.

If you are endlessly arguing about the same subject, look hard at it. Is it something that can't be resolved and which you will both have to learn to live with? If so, you need to agree to differ and deal with your own feelings about it in an adult way. Consider the following example: Your partner doesn't like your mother, but you want him to like her. This can't be resolved quickly, if at all, although when and how you see your mother can. Accept your partner's feelings, and deal with your own hurt and disappointment in an adult way, perhaps by talking to a friend, writing about it in a journal or booking a session with a counsellor.

Perhaps your regular argument is about something that can be resolved simply, such as who is responsible for certain household tasks or how to manage money. Choose a time when you are both in a good mood to sit down and sort out solutions (see also Negotiating Skills, page 210).

Make sure arguments are not damaging your relationship.

STEP EIGHT: LETTING GO

Today is the day to focus on cultivating a skill which will be enormously useful in creating a strong and happy relationship - the ability to let things go. Learning to walk away from conflict and to feel that whatever's at stake really doesn't matter too much will put your relationship on a firm foundation. It sounds simple, so why can't we do it all the time? In a conflict, we almost always have a big investment in being right. We are convinced that if we can only get the other person to see our point of view they will have to concede. The trouble is, they usually feel the same way, which leads to conflicts, arguments, discord and so on.

EXERCISE

Think of your last three arguments. Who was right? Do you believe it was you? Now ask your partner the same question; he will probably say it was actually him.

The solution to this apparently no-win situation is simply to let go of the need to be right. This becomes easier when you realize that there is seldom an absolute right and wrong, but only different points of view. If you asked a hundred people at random about your argument, half of them might agree with you and half might agree with your partner. Also remember that most conflicts seem unimportant a few hours or days later. So what if your partner had his hair cut too short (in your opinion) or if you packed too many clothes in the suitcase (in his opinion)? After all, it hardly matters in the great scheme of things.

LETTING GO

* When your partner upsets you, take a deep breath and count to ten. Or try to put some space between you for half an hour or so.

* Persuade yourself that this probably won't matter in a few days' time.

* If possible, look for a funny side to the argument - if you both start laughing, it will release the tension.

* Decide to be generous and let your partner be right. If you can say: "Okay, you win, let's stop now," he'll be so surprised that he may well decide you were right after all.

* Agree to postpone the argument while you both do something else. Reschedule it to a couple of hours later - chances are you'll no longer want to.

* Say: "Let's both be right", and hug.

* Tell yourself that people who are right all the time can be infuriating. Do you want to be one of them?

* Learn how to feel indignant without needing to start World War III. Let off steam in a hot bath, then reassess the issue when you feel calmer.

* Think about something wonderful - the best sex you ever had together, the holiday you are planning - to remind yourself how much you love each other.

* Tell yourself that if you win the argument, an hour later you will feel smug and self-satisfied - and miserable. And you probably won't be speaking to one another. But if you let it go, in an hour you'll be glad you did.

> Learn to let things go and be a winner every time.

STEP NINE: NEGOTIATING SKILLS

Polish your negotiating skills today - they'll prove invaluable for your relationship. Many people think that negotiation is really about beating the other person into the ground, making him or her give in and getting your own way. This is actually more like bulldozing and doesn't leave anyone (even the winner) feeling good. Negotiation is about compromise, but it is also about creating a win-win situation in which you both come away feeling that you have made your point, gained something and felt good about yourself at the same time.

Although vital to living with and loving another person, negotiation is only possible if you believe that you are both entitled to a satisfying solution. Failing to negotiate leads to bitterness and resentment. The relationship will be out of balance and won't function well or be happy if things go all your way or all your partner's.

To begin, you must be willing to state your position, stand up for your rights and defend your case firmly but flexibly - which means giving up playing victim or persecutor. When you feel sorry for yourself, expect to be argued down or constantly give in, you are playing the role of the victim; when you steamroller your partner, behave aggressively or expect to come out on top every time, you become the persecutor. Neither of these roles is much fun either to play or to be around. Instead, choose to be adult and negotiate.

Guidelines for Good Negotiation

* Choose a time when you are both in a reasonably good mood.

* Make sure that there won't be any interruptions, from children or telephone calls, for instance.

* Sit at a table. This helps you feel more adult and businesslike, and ensures that you are both on the same level; avoid one person sitting and the other standing.

* Take turns to put forward your case, making sure that you really LISTEN to one another.

* Be willing to concede some points.

* Know your bottom line, the limit beyond which you won't bargain.

* Put all possible solutions on the table.

* If the discussion gets heated, take a break and come back later.

* Search for a solution that you can both live with and which gives each of you part of what you want.

* If the solution doesn't work, be willing to come back to the table and try to find a different one.

Of course, there will always be non-negotiable points, and you have to decide what these are. However, negotiating on more flexible or less clear-cut issues (and most things can be seen in shades of grey, rather than black and white) can prove mutually rewarding and revealing.

Choose to believe that a solution can always be found.

STEP TEN: SORT OUT SEX

Good sex is part of a good relationship. To be lovers as well as friends, you need sex, and if the sex is going wrong the rest of the relationship will suffer, too. Sex is an important ingredient of romantic love, so it's worth devoting time and effort to it.

EXERCISE

How would you rate your sex life, on a scale from 1 to 10? If it's 8 or above, that's great - think of today as a refresher course. Any lower, though, and there is definite room for improvement.

First, identify what's going wrong. Here are some common symptoms of a less-than-satisfactory sex life. Do any of these scenarios sound familiar?

☐ You are not satisfied, you don't have orgasms, or you have orgasms but not much fun before or after them.

☐ Sex is always the same old routine, and you are bored.

☐ Your partner doesn't really know how to turn you on.

☐ You are not attracted to your partner, or you feel he isn't attracted to you.

☐ One of you is too tired - or you both are.

☐ Children always seem to interrupt.

☐ You've never really enjoyed sex.

☐ There's always too much on your mind.

☐ There are some things you don't like doing in bed, which upsets your partner so that you both become tense.

If so, don't worry: sex often proves an easy area to improve. If you have had good sex in the past, you know how marvellous it can be, and it's just a question of rediscovering it. And if sex has never been great for the two of you, now's the time to make it so. Loving and caring for each other will enable you to have great sex. In fact, the more relaxed and familiar you are with one another, the better the sex can be. Sex can become boring with time - if you let it - but it can also get better and better ...

HOW TO HAVE GREAT SEX

Get the scene right
Agree not to argue or discuss big issues in the bedroom - keep talk warm and loving there. Make the room a beautiful place to be, with soft sheets, candles, scents and so on.

Enjoy the build-up
Bathing together is nice and making love to someone who is fresh and clean is even nicer. Watch a sexy video (not porn, just a bit of lust) if you like, or a funny movie, because laughing relaxes you and makes you feel happy.

Put worries, stress and children beyond the bedroom door
And don't let them in - use a lock on the door if possible.

Start slowly
Try massaging, stroking or kissing each other all over ...

Think sexy and you'll feel sexy
The sexiest part of you is your brain, so use fantasies of the best sex you've ever had or of making love in outrageous places to stimulate your body's responses.

Talk
Tell your partner how sexy he is, how much you fancy him and how much you like what he's doing (when you do). In return, ask what he enjoys - and do it.

Experiment
Without doing anything that makes you feel uncomfortable, explore new territory, such as role-playing or different positions.

Ignore tiredness

Once you make the effort, sex can actually restore your energy if you are tired, and it will help you sleep better afterwards!

Decide today to make your sex life the best it can be and to think of your partner as the sexiest person in the world, now and for ever.

Great sex can be a wonderful part of a great relationship.

STEP ELEVEN: KEEP THE LAUGHTER FLOWING

Never forget the power of laughter: relationships run more smoothly and happily with a hefty dose of humour thrown in. Laughter works like magic. The simple act of moving your facial muscles into a smile or a laugh, even if you don't feel like doing it, has an astonishing effect. It causes your brain to release "feel good" hormones, which then flood your body, making you feel better, lighter and happier.

EXERCISE

Try this today. Smile at everyone you meet. Not only will it make you feel better, but you will also receive a warmer response from others.

In a relationship, laughter can break a deadlock, lighten a grim mood, stop an argument and improve sex. Laughter heals hurts and brings you closer. The more you laugh, the more you lighten up, and that's good for all aspects of life. If either of you is a worrier or prone to anxiety, laughing can help alleviate the stresses.

How to bring more laughter into your life:

* Go to a comedy club or watch comedy programmes on television.

* Read a humorous novel.

* Tickle each other (if you both like it).

* Share any good jokes you have heard.

* Remember and relate funny stories you heard or read, or experiences you had during the day.

* Keep videos that made you laugh and play them when you need a lift.

* Be willing to see the funny side of anything, especially sex.

Often the lighter side of life is overshadowed when couples settle down together. Suddenly bills, children and responsibilities swamp them and laughter evaporates.

Little children laugh dozens of times a day. Be more like them and find a lot to laugh about. Be playful with one another, too. Have pillow fights, chase each other in the park, fool around when you have the chance. Everyone loves to be around people who take life lightly. Taking life lightly means knowing that whatever happens isn't the end of the world; it means keeping perspective and trusting that it will all come right. Life should never be so serious that there's no room for laughter.

For a happy, harmonious relationship, keep laughing.

STEP TWELVE: ANGER

Think about the role of anger in your relationship. Everyone gets angry from time to time, and we each deal with it in different ways. Many people feel uncomfortable with their anger, or other people's, and it may bring up deep-seated fears and tensions. Perhaps you weren't allowed to be angry when you were a child because your parents disapproved of displays of anger and you learnt to hide it. But hiding anger doesn't make it disappear - it just leaks out in other ways.

How do you deal with anger? Do any of these responses sound familiar?

☐ You pretend you aren't angry, suppressing it, but end up exploding later.

☐ You hold it in and become ill as a result.

☐ You turn anger into resentment and walk around feeling like a martyr.

☐ You let it leak out gradually in bursts of criticism and irritation.

☐ You wait until anger has built up to the point where you shout and scream.

Almost all of us do one or more of the above at some point, and many of us do them often. But dealing with anger in these ways is not much fun and can be very destructive, so make the decision today to try a different approach.

COPING WITH ANGER IN POSITIVE WAYS

Tell yourself that it's okay to be angry
Anger is just a feeling, like any other, and you can't stop yourself feeling angry any more than you can stop yourself feeling lonely or sad. The important thing is how you BEHAVE when you feel angry.

216

Don't behave badly when you are angry
If you do, you will make yourself miserable. Choose not to shout, scream, sulk, carp, criticize or slam doors.

Do something constructive
Sometimes it's enough simply to acknowledge your anger, telling yourself, "I'm really angry about . . ." You could also try the following: shut yourself in the car and scream; write an angry letter but don't send it; write in a journal; punch a pillow; or exercise.

Anger can be a sign that something needs to change
If this is the case, identify what it is and begin taking steps to change it.

Remember that feelings follow behaviour
When you change your actions, your mood will follow. Sometimes the fastest way out of an angry frame of mind is to alter your behaviour. Go for a walk, dance, do anything you find fun, and your anger will subside.

Express your anger appropriately
Sometimes you need your partner to know that you are angry and to act differently. Try this approach: simply and clearly state why you are angry, tell your partner how the behaviour makes you feel, then say exactly what you would like your partner to do.

To defuse potentially explosive situations, always be specific, rather than general, and avoid insults. Use "I" statements rather than "you" statements. For example, don't say: "You always attack me in front of my friends, you're a nasty, thoughtless creep." Do say: "I was really hurt tonight when you made that comment in front of our friends. I'd like you to treat me with respect and talk to me politely." Your partner is then far more likely to listen and do what you want.

> Let go of your fears, and use anger as a tool for positive change.

STEP THIRTEEN: FRIENDS

When we begin a committed relationship, there is always some adjusting to do in our friendships. Sometimes friends welcome the relationship, but sometimes they don't; they may willingly take a back seat, or they may not. Friends are precious, and keeping them when you enter into a romantic relationship is important, but it's equally important not to let them dominate or sabotage the relationship. A careful balance needs to be reached between your partner and your friends.

Are your friends more important to you than your partner? Are they intruding into relationship territory?

Here are some warning signs:

* You regularly ask your best friend for advice about the relationship, then follow it.

* You discuss intimate details of the relationship with a friend, things you know your partner would be uncomfortable about you divulging.

* You prefer an evening with a friend to an evening with your partner.

* You often cancel plans with your partner because a friend has a problem (however minor) and wants advice.

If any of the above ring true for you, listen to the warning bells: three in a relationship doesn't work. A friend this closely involved is almost certain to be undermining your relationship. Friends like this are seldom supportive of the relationship; they may be jealous and want you all to themselves.

GETTING THE BALANCE RIGHT

Remember that your partner comes first. He or she needs to be the person who matters most in your life. The two of you are a unit, and the people around you need to know that they can't possibly divide you.

Keep friendships within clear boundaries. Friends don't come on dates with the two of you and don't take priority over your arrangements with your partner, unless there is a genuine crisis.

Stop discussing the more intimate aspects of the relationship with your friends.

Some things between you and your partner should stay private - instinct will tell you what these are.

The balance, though not always easy to achieve, is crucial. Friends need to know that they matter to you and that you will be there for them, but at the same time make it clear to everyone that your partner comes first. Always remember that a true friend will respect and encourage a relationship that makes you happy and will gladly step back to make room for your partner.

There is room in your life for both your partner and friends.

STEP FOURTEEN: FAMILY

After friends, it's time to look at the role of family - yours and your partner's - in the relationship. Some of the advice on friendships (see page 218) also applies to family, but there are other more complex and subtle ways in which families can interfere in relationships. Be on the lookout for these and nip them in the bud. No matter how precious your mother, father, sister or brother, they are not the person who will live with you, share decisions and choices, and shape a life together. They have their own lives and need to take a back seat in yours. Your family may be deeply important to you, but your relationship is most important of all - it is about your future.

How families, especially parents, can undermine the relationship:

* Criticizing your partner in subtle, or not so subtle, ways.

* Giving constant advice on how to run your relationship, home, life and so on.

* Offering money to you or your partner in a way that upsets the balance of the relationship.

* Demanding an impossible degree of attention.

* Bribing you (or your partner) to leave the relationship; for example, by promising an inheritance.

* Competing with you; for example, it is not uncommon for a man's mother to compete with his new partner.

* Bullying.

* Insisting that the relationship won't last.

If any of the above are threatening your relationship, it's time to take action. Be absolutely sure that the role of family members is to be supportive and encouraging, offering help or advice with sensitivity or only when asked. Be firm about setting boundaries and resisting their interference. This can be done without causing dramas or estrangement. Simply smile and say: "Thank you, but no", or brush criticism aside, while making it clear that your relationship is solid and strong.

Interfering relatives can, and often do, destroy a relationship. Of course, there are times when parents or family members have genuine concerns about a specific problem. If this is the case, thank them for their concern and decide for yourself what action to take.

Always remember that the relationship is your decision. You don't need anyone else's permission or approval for your choice of partner. If the relationship is right for you, that's all that matters. As an adult you get to celebrate your own successes and deal with your problems and mistakes.

> Make it clear to family members that your relationship comes first.

STEP FIFTEEN: TRUST

To have a successful relationship you need to be able to trust one another, and to trust one another, you need to behave in a way that is trustworthy. Trust without foundation only leads to hurt and disillusion. Trusting someone the minute you meet him, though you may have a strong instinct that he is trustworthy and want to follow it, is inappropriate. Even if you feel this way, go slowly. Wait until you know that the person is truly as trustworthy as you hoped he would be before you invest your trust in him.

Many people trust too soon and get hurt. Others stay suspicious and refuse to trust, even when they are with someone who is clearly worthy of trust. When this happens, they are bringing their lack of trust from the past into the present.

How do you know whether someone is worthy of trust?

Here are some signs to look for:

Does your partner do what he says he will do?

This is the most important indicator of trustworthiness. You have a right to expect someone who says he will phone on a certain day or at a certain time to keep his word. The same applies to everything else your partner says he will do.

If your partner is always too ready with excuses, be warned.

Unreliability is immature, selfish and often a sign of deeper untrustworthiness.

Does your partner have secrets?

If he won't tell you things about himself, or behaves in a secretive way, ask yourself what he might want to hide.

Behaving in a trustworthy way yourself is important. You can't expect to attract someone worth trusting unless you are worth trusting, too. Make sure that you act in an open, honest, consistent, reliable and fair way.

If you believe that your partner is behaving in an untrustworthy way, you must decide whether you will accept this or not. Explain your worries and fears, and don't invest trust until you know that this is the right thing to do. However, be alert to the danger of being overly suspicious. If you are refusing to trust someone who is behaving in a clear and open way, then you need to make changes. Recognize that your doubts belong in the past, with some other situation or person. Perhaps someone else - a parent, for instance - abandoned you and now your fear of abandonment is holding the relationship back. Look at your partner with fresh eyes and be willing to trust where trust has been earned.

Always behave
in a way that is
worthy of trust.

STEP SIXTEEN: APPRECIATION

So often we begin a relationship full of appreciation, noticing the little things a lover does for us and loving everything about him. Then, all too soon, we get used to one another, the special things become ordinary and appreciation is lost. Today, remind yourself of all there is to appreciate in your partner and the relationship.

Appreciation is about making people feel good about themselves, counting your blessings and focusing on all that is good. Sometimes we notice and appreciate, but we don't say anything. Voicing your appreciation and letting your partner know what you value and appreciate about him is always a good move in a relationship. If you notice, and comment on, the ways in which your partner is kind, generous, brave, supportive and encouraging, the qualities you love about him, he will feel cherished. Learning to appreciate can also help you find the good in any situation and turn potentially difficult or unhappy situations around.

EXERCISE

List ten things you appreciate about your partner. Have fun with the list, adding more as you think of them. You might include:

* Qualities, such as generosity, loyalty, courage or humour.

* Talents, such as being a great lover or cook.

* Developed skills, such as rock-climbing or an advanced degree.

* Commitment to the relationship.

* How he takes responsibility for aspects of his life.

* Hard work.

* Dress sense.

* Appearance or voice.

* Sensitivity in difficult situations.

* Willingness to support you, emotionally and/or financially.

....

....

....

....

....

....

....

Now make a second list of qualities that you appreciate about yourself, because this is just as important as appreciating your partner.

....

....

....

....

....

....

....

Make a third list of aspects of the relationship and the way the two of you are together that you appreciate, adding to them as they occur to you. You might include:

* The way you have stuck together through problems and rough patches.

* How you both deal with arguments and find resolutions.

* The laughter and fun in the relationship.

* Your ability to balance being together with the other demands in life.

* Romantic gestures you make to one another.

* The way you put one another first.

* Mutual contributions to running the home.

* Willingness to be flexible about decisions.

* Responsibilities each of you take in your joint life.

* The support you give one another in doing what matters to each of you.

....

....

....

....

....

....

....

....

....

As you write the lists you will be surprised by how much you are grateful for.

Make appreciation a habit from now on. Every step, find three things to admire about your partner and make sure you communicate them.

Appreciation is the
key to goodwill
and happiness.

STEP SEVENTEEN: MONEY MATTERS

All too often, money becomes a problem between a couple and a major source of arguments and tensions, and this isn't surprising. When you enter a relationship, you each take all kinds of money issues and attitudes with you. One partner's point of view can be very different to the other's. A compromise has to be found and common ground negotiated, and for this you need plenty of tolerance and goodwill.

Examples of different attitudes to money:

* One of you thinks the other spends far too much, or thinks the other person is mean.

* One partner earns more and resents being the major breadwinner.

* One partner earns much less and feels inferior or resents being dependent.

* One of you hates figures and leaves the other to take charge of the accounting.

* One of you thinks all will work out in the end, while the other worries and frets.

* Priorities can't be agreed between the two of you; for example, you want a mortgage, but your partner wants extra holidays, or he wants to save while you want to eat out more often.

The answer to all these problems - and any others that you have identified - is a blend of compromise, understanding and negotiation.

HOW TO SOLVE MONEY ISSUES

* No matter who earns the most, you should both have an equal say about joint spending issues. The bigger earner doesn't have more clout in this case.

* Agree from the start to listen to and respect one another's point of view.

* Sit down, in peace and quiet, and in a good mood, and put all the money issues and decisions on the table.

* Go through each issue one by one, taking turns to have your say. Look for areas of compromise. For example, could you save a little more and still go out to dinner reasonably often? Could you opt for a smaller mortgage and manage one extra holiday (perhaps a weekend break) each year?

* Agree who is in charge of book-keeping and plan to meet regularly - weekly or monthly - to keep up to date on finances and make decisions for the future.

* Make sure that you both have your own money, as well as a joint fund. Ideally, keep separate accounts, plus a joint account for household expenses.

* Agree that neither of you can comment on how the other chooses to spend personal money. Only the money in the joint account is up for negotiation.

The key to resolving money tensions is to keep everything open, uncomplicated and clear. Be willing to find a compromise to any problem, however insoluble it seems.

Don't let money come between you - ever.

STEP EIGHTEEN: LOOK AFTER YOURSELF

Today you need to focus on the way you look after yourself in the relationship. Women, especially, often concentrate all their energies on their partners, but of course this can happen the other way around, too. When all your attention and energy is expended on the other person, you neglect your own needs and desires. What happens then is almost always bad for both of you.

Just as you are trying to meet your partner's needs and give him everything he wants, so you expect your partner to look after you and give you what you want. This can be a recipe for disaster. As you discover your needs aren't being met, you get whiny, resentful and needy, which makes you steadily less attractive. Your partner, feeling under pressure, wants to run a mile. In fact, the pressure on your partner is doubled: he has you trying to please him, which can feel like a big burden, and then has the added pressure of being expected to look after you. In your efforts to please your partner, you are actually making him (and yourself) miserable.

If this is happening in your relationship, be honest and recognize that it's time to stop. This scenario can break a relationship very quickly, and that's sad because there is no need for it.

EXERCISE

Break the needy/pleasing cycle. Start developing your "selfish" muscle. Being selfish can be a good thing because it means learning to look after your own needs and wants without expecting someone else to fulfil them for you.

Sit down, right now, and ask yourself: "What do I want?"

List ten things you want which you would normally do without or hope that your partner would provide. For instance, you might want to have time to read or paint; to have a cup of tea in bed in the morning, a foot massage or a special dinner; or to redecorate the home. Getting the hang of working out what you want can take a while, so add to the list as you think of more.

How many things on the list could you provide for yourself? Probably all of them. Begin right now, today, with something you can do for yourself. Make this a habit: every time you feel grumpy, critical or sorry for yourself, think about something that you really want and either give it to yourself or plan to as soon as possible.

Stop doing everything for your partner. Give up trying to anticipate what your partner wants or trying to fix things for him. Stand back and let him sort things out for himself.

Behave towards one another in a caring way, but don't overdo it or caring can become smothering and overwhelming. The antidote to smothering behaviour is to keep bringing the spotlight back to you. The more you put the spotlight on your own needs, the less you will put it on your partner's. Every time you are tempted to fuss and do something for your partner which he doesn't really need you to do, do something for yourself instead. A huge amount of pressure on the relationship will be eased and you will be a lot more fun to be around.

Look after yourself
as well, and your
relationship will thrive.

STEP NINETEEN: ASK FOR WHAT YOU WANT

After learning to look after yourself, the next step forward is to learn to ask for what you want. So many relationships would be much easier if couples would only ask rather than expect the other to guess. What you think is obvious (that you want a hug, for example) probably isn't obvious at all. So when your partner does what he thinks you want instead (perhaps leaving you alone instead of hugging you), you feel upset and angry. Your partner can't understand what he did wrong and the spiral of disappointment continues. Wouldn't it have been so much simpler if you had just asked for a hug in the first place?

WHY DON'T MOST OF US ASK FOR WHAT WE WANT?

Here are some of the reasons:

* We don't know what we want so we can't ask for it.

* We're afraid we won't get it.

* We think we don't deserve it.

* We think we've got to earn it by pleasing the other person first.

* We think it won't be special if we've had to ask for it.

Do any of these apply to you? Very few people know how to ask for what they want, regularly, and feel good about it. Most of us have a big resistance to asking. But just like any other kind of behaviour, requesting what you want is a habit you can cultivate, simply by being willing to do it over and over again until it feels easy and familiar.

HOW TO ASK FOR WHAT YOU WANT

* Remember that people who love you are usually more than willing to give you what you want, if they can.

* Consider some of the things you want - chances are they are really quite simple.

* Practise asking in a direct but warm way. Avoid whining, pleading, cajoling or flattering.

* Be willing to settle for SOME of what you want. Abandon the idea that you have to have it all.

* Remember that it's a real relief for the other person when you say what you want. He can stop guessing, and this saves a lot of energy and grief.

* If your partner says no, accept that the answer is not a rejection of you, but that they simply can't do it, for his own reasons.

* Learn how to receive graciously. When you do get what you want, show him how appreciative you are and then enjoy it. Don't use it as an excuse to trigger off a guilt trip or decide you have to give your partner double what he has just given you.

Sometimes receiving can be a lot harder than giving, so remind yourself that you deserve it and relax. Once you both get the hang of it, asking for what you want can bring you closer - so go on, give it a try.

Be brave and generous, and ask for what you want.

STEP TWENTY: ALWAYS BE YOU

Too often, in a relationship, we lose track of who we are. We are so busy focusing on the other person or on being part of a couple that suddenly we can't find our own identity. A successful relationship is not about being half of a whole, but about two wholes coming together in harmony. So it's important to keep your individual identity strong and not to feel that something of the essential you has been lost or smothered.

Signs of loss of identity. Do any of these ring true?

☐ You can't make decisions about anything, even which film you'd like to see, without consulting your partner.

☐ You feel weird going to social events on your own.

☐ You never arrange to do things without him if you can help it.

☐ You always shop together.

☐ If your partner is away for a night, you panic.

☐ You don't enjoy your own company.

☐ You've stopped doing things that you used to enjoy because your partner doesn't want to do them.

☐ You would rather be with him than without him, even if it means going to an event or joining in an activity you don't like.

☐ You use the word "we" more often than the word "I".

☐ You can't imagine life without your partner; if he died, you'd have to die, too.

Are you so immersed in coupledom that the mere thought of being just "me" or "I" makes you feel afraid and lonely? If so, it's time to stop subsuming your identity in your partner's. You can learn to stand on your own two feet without losing the closeness you share.

BEING YOURSELF WHILE STAYING IN LOVE

* Nurture friendships that are just yours. Make dates to see your friends regularly, without your partner.

* Set aside time to do what you enjoy. Spend at least one night a week on an activity that you enjoy - yoga, photography, or going to see a movie with friends - and which doesn't involve your partner.

* Exercise your decision-making and opinion "muscles". Frequently ask yourself: "What do I think about this?", "What would I like to do now" or "What kind of evening out would suit me?" This doesn't mean you always have to have your way, but helps you to know what you think and want.

* Make sure that there are times when you don't think or talk about your partner. Don't go out with friends and then talk only about your partner; instead, discuss life, politics, fashion, books, music - anything that helps you branch out.

* Don't automatically do everything with him. If you bathe together too often, it may stop being special. Keep the buzz by rationing some of the things you do together so that they remain special rather than routine.

* Don't do what your partner wants to do just to be with him. If asked to go along to a football match or a yoga class, don't trail along if you don't actually enjoy it.

Do something you like instead.

Keep your life interesting and it will keep you interesting, too. Make sure that you always have enough to talk about and that you do some things on your own. Never take togetherness too far.

Always believe that if you lost your partner, you would be strong enough to go on with a fulfilling, enriching life. No couples know how long they have together, but believing that you would cope alone will make you happier and stronger now.

Be yourself and stay whole and happy.

STEP TWENTY-ONE: KNOW YOUR BOUNDARIES

A boundary is like a limit: it is a line that should not be crossed, a point which is as far as you can comfortably go. In relationships, just as in life, we need boundaries. They help us feel safe, comfortable and whole, and they define who we are. Boundaries are neither good nor bad. Everyone's are different and we choose them simply because they feel right for us. Whether we are aware of them or not, we all have them. However, many of us have weak or absent boundaries in certain areas, and this can lead to feelings of being easily overwhelmed and stressed.

SIGNS OF WEAK OR MISSING BOUNDARIES

* You decide on an activity, but then change your mind because your partner asks you to do something else.

  For example, you are planning a night in, reading a good book, until your partner asks you to go out; you don't want to go, but you do anyway.

* You make a mutual rule or promise, but then break it or ignore your partner breaking it. For example, you decide not to take telephone calls after midnight. You tell your partner, then answer the telephone as usual when a friend calls at 1 am a few days later. Or, you promise to stop smoking, but then carry on.

* You decide that certain behaviour is unacceptable, but then accept it. For example, you tell your partner that you will leave if he hits you, then stay after you've been hit again.

EXERCISE

Try to define your boundaries, establishing new ones if you need them, then make a promise to keep them in place. You don't need hundreds - too many can be as bad as too few - but the ones you do put in place must be the right and important ones for you.

When fixing boundaries, remember a couple of points. Firstly, other people will always test your boundaries. If you hold the line, they will respect you and know that you mean what you say; if you don't, they will know you're a pushover. Secondly, be prepared to stick to your boundaries; don't make one you know you're going to break, as you will feel that you can't trust yourself.

For these two reasons, choose boundaries that are important enough to keep. For example, pick an issue that has been bothering you and decide where the boundary needs to be. You will soon discover how good it feels to stick to your decision, even when your partner tests you by trying to break it.

> Keep your boundaries and trust yourself to mean what you say.

STEP TWENTY-TWO: RESPONSIBILITY

To keep love strong, both partners in a relationship need to be responsible. If your reaction to this is, "How boring, that sounds dull and worthy", think again. Being responsible doesn't just mean paying your bills and buying the groceries - it runs far deeper than that.

True love entails being willing to take responsibility. This means acting in a consistent and appropriate way, and when we do this we create deep and meaningful bonds. Few things kill love faster than a total lack of responsibility on the part of either partner; if you have ever been affected by this, you will know how true it is. Those who behave irresponsibly are willing to let others down, to burden others, to use others as cover, to create problems and to cause hurt. There is no place for any of this in a strong and healthy relationship. Take a look at your relationship. Are you being irresponsible or putting up with your partner's irresponsible behaviour?

STRENGTHENING YOUR LEVELS OF RESPONSIBILITY

* Always behave in a way of which you can be proud. Identify areas of behaviour that cause you shame and clean them up.

* Remember that love and responsibility go together. You can't claim to love someone without being willing to behave responsibly towards them.

* Responsibility begins with yourself. Are you looking after and nurturing yourself? Are you getting enough rest, good food and exercise? You won't be able to respond appropriately to the demands of life and your relationship unless you are fulfilling the basic responsibilities to yourself.

* Behaving responsibly towards your partner means doing what you've said you'll do and keeping your half of any agreements

made. It doesn't mean fussing, fixing or smothering your partner. Sometimes the responsible act is to step back and let him sort out his own mess.

* When deciding what your responsibilities are, the key word is "appropriate". Use this as a measure to ensure that you don't overdo it.

IF THE IRRESPONSIBLE PERSON IS YOUR PARTNER

* Let your partner feel the consequences of his actions. In other words, don't always cover up for him, rescue him from fixes of his own making or do something that he really should do for himself. Stand back and let him deal with whatever happens.

* Make your own boundaries clear. Let your partner know what you will and won't do and what you expect from him. Don't drone on - just say it once, then leave it.

* Decide whether you really want to be around someone who is consistently irresponsible. You may want to withdraw, partially or wholly, rather than live with behaviour that causes problems for you.

* If the irresponsibility is just in specific areas, tackle them by making the consequences clear. For example, if your partner always arrives very late to meet you, let him know that you will wait ten minutes before leaving.

Tackling irresponsibility is an exciting challenge. It means being willing to stand up and be counted, to set your boundaries and to acknowledge the powerful connection between responsibility and love.

Be responsible and feel good about who you are.

STEP TWENTY-THREE: THE GREEN-EYED MONSTER

Jealousy is undermining and destructive. Everyone is jealous from time to time, but consistent jealousy causes deep rifts in a relationship. Today is the day to examine the role jealousy plays in your relationship. Are you or your partner consistently jealous? Is jealousy an issue between you? If so, it's time to do something about it.

If either of you is experiencing feelings of jealousy, ask yourself: "Is there a reason?" Is one of you causing it by behaving inappropriately? Sometimes all the blame is laid on the partner who is jealous when the other partner has played a part in the problem. Are you both behaving in a trustworthy and appropriate way (see Trust, page 221)? Are you putting your partner first, not flirting or spending too much time with other people, and treating one another with care, respect and consideration? Tackle these areas and the jealousy should disappear. If jealousy continues to be a problem, the root cause may be insecurity and low self-esteem (see also Respect Yourself, page 203).

HOW TO DEAL WITH YOUR JEALOUSY

Begin to build up your self-esteem and sense of self-worth
The stronger these are, the less jealous you will be. Talk to yourself in positive ways, appreciate all the good in what you are and what you do and be kind to yourself.

Talk to your partner about the problem
Ask for his support in dealing with it and discuss particular triggers for your jealousy - your partner may be able to offer help at these times.

List all the reasons why you are loved
Reassure yourself that you are lovable, worthwhile and worthy of your partner.

Make the decision to stop being jealous
Refuse to let anything be bigger than you or beyond your control - the relationship is too precious to damage or lose.

When you feel jealousy rising, do something different
Focus on times when you've felt great about yourself and, if need be, remove yourself from the situation until the jealousy has gone.

Tackling jealousy in these ways, firmly and consistently, will enable you to control it. If your partner is jealous, offer to support him in every reasonable and appropriate way, as long as he is willing to deal with his feelings, too. Encourage your partner to feel good about himself and to feel loved. Often jealousy is a passing phase. Plenty of couples have found it a problem at some stage, but have dealt with it successfully, so take heart.

Don't let jealousy damage the love between you.

STEP TWENTY-FOUR: SLOW AND SURE

For this step, focus on the importance of taking your time in all things connected with love and relationships. Are you madly in love? Longing to rush into living together, marriage and children? Or are you further down the line and moving very quickly into lifestyle changes which affect both of you? If you are speeding ahead in the relationship, or you recognize that rushing into things is your tendency, devote today to thinking about slowing down and discovering the benefits this brings.

The consequences of haste in a relationship can be immense - and often negative. More mistakes are made when we rush into decisions and there is less time to deal with any effects or feelings that arise. Most importantly, take time when deciding to marry. There is no need to rush into it if you are going to stay together, is there? The divorce courts are full of couples who say: "We went into it too fast and then found we didn't know one another and were too different." Few people say: "We went into it too slowly, we were just too thoughtful and careful, and we took too long to get to know one another." Committing to another person for life is the most exciting and challenging decision you will ever take, so be as sure as you can that it is the right one for both of you.

Don't commit if you want to:

* Change anything significant about your partner. It is very hard to make someone stop drinking/like your friends/want a baby or anything else, and it will put a great strain on the marriage.

* Escape from another situation - in order to get away from overprotective parents or another unhappy relationship, for example. Instead, move into a marriage from a clear, secure, happy space.

* Get to know your partner better. If you don't already know them very, very well, it's not time to commit.

* Solve a problem, such as dodgy finances or fear of being left on the shelf.

* Stop the nagging. Never agree to marry just to shut your partner (or anyone else) up, and don't agree just to please them - it is rarely wise in the long run.

The time to commit is when:

* You know your partner inside out, bad habits and all, and still adore him.

* You trust him completely and are sure he will be faithful and reliable.

* You can take the decision independently of anyone else's input.

* You have dealt with any major problems. Some little ones are bound to remain, but the big ones - such as excessive drinking or infidelity, lifestyle differences or whether to have children or not - need to be resolved.

Follow the same general "don't rush" rules for any major aspect of your lives together, and it's wise to apply them to the small things in life as well. Live in haste, racing from one thing to another, and you'll find stress is overwhelming the relationship.

Take your time to make sure that your decisions are right for you.

STEP TWENTY-FIVE: HAPPINESS

Today, simply be happy. Not when, if or because, but right now, just for its own sake. Too often we rely on the other person in our relationship to make us feel happy or we wait for happiness to come along, like a bus, and solve everything. We may believe that once all our problems are solved (though they never are), we'll feel happy. If you find yourself saying: "We'd be happy if ..." or "If he'd just ... I'd be so happy", give it up right now! Whatever is stopping you from being happy, refuse to let it. Happiness is a state of mind and nothing will ever make you more happy than simply deciding to be so. Take the active decision to be responsible for your own happiness and to choose it over unhappiness on a daily basis.

HOW TO STAY HAPPY IN A RELATIONSHIP

Think happy thoughts
This requires a conscious effort on your part to choose thoughts that make you feel good and to combat unhappy, negative thoughts. Inner thoughts are like living beings, powerful, active and influential, so think carefully about which ones you allow in.

Nurture good feelings for your partner
Make this a priority. Relationships begin with a lot of warmth and love. If there is less now, then aim to raise the level by concentrating on positive feelings and behaving in a warm and loving way. When you feel warmth for your partner, your relationship feels good.

Be cautious of low moods
When you are feeling down and miserable, you may begin to pick holes in everything in your life and nothing will seem right or good enough. Resist this: simply comfort yourself or ask your partner for comfort, and wait for the mood to pass.

Remember that your life is your choice
And so is how you react to whatever comes. Try not to let things get the better of you. Instead, take charge of life. If you don't like the choices you've made, change them. If troubles strike, know that you will survive them, on your own or with others' support.

Repeat a positive mantra to yourself
Start every day by saying: "Today I am willing to allow happiness into my life. I welcome it with open arms. I choose to be happy."

Don't dwell on problems and setbacks
Take downturns as lightly as possible, don't let them trigger arguments and actively look for a solution to every problem.

To be happy in a relationship you need to cultivate happiness in yourself. Hold on tightly to the knowledge that you have a choice. Why be miserable when you can choose to be happy?

Let happiness be a way of living and loving.

STEP TWENTY-SIX: ACCEPTANCE

A big part of settling into a long-term relationship is accepting the other person. There will always be changes you want to make, aspects of the person that bother or irritate you, or habits you don't like or don't understand. Acknowledge that you are never going to like everything about your partner all of the time. Liking most things most of the time is doing pretty well. Accept those things you dislike in your partner (within reason) and let them go.

Focusing too much attention on the aspects you don't like will inevitably cause problems. An unimportant habit that irritates you - such as biting his nails, phoning his mother every day or leaving his clothes on the floor - can escalate into a reason to hate him if you let it. Any other feelings of discontent, resentment and anger you have will feed the irritation about your partner's habit until it becomes overwhelming.

Why do we find it so hard to accept someone just as they are? Partly because we enter a relationship with certain expectations, then try to get the person we've chosen to fit those expectations. Instead of waiting patiently, with genuine curiosity, to find out who they are, we look for signs that they will fit the ready-made mould we've already designed.

KEYS TO ACCEPTANCE

Accept that you can't change another person
If he wants to change, you can certainly help him, but trying to change someone who isn't interested in changing will leave you frustrated, let down and helpless. Sometimes asking the person, kindly and specifically, to change a particular behaviour or habit works if he has the goodwill to do it, but that's as far as changing someone else can go.

Recognize that the only person you can change is yourself
Usually when we transform ourselves in some way, other people change their response to us. So if you want your partner to stop treating you like a doormat, stop behaving like one. If you want less arguing in the relationship, take responsibility for your side of the rows and stop. If you want your partner to open up and talk to you, tell him about your own feelings and be willing to really listen to his.

Focus on the positive
Concentrate on all you love about your partner and decide that you can live with a few irritating habits.

Take the focus off the source of irritation
Try laughing about it and telling yourself: "Oh, well, so what if he leaves the bathroom in a mess/is always losing his car keys, it doesn't matter."

Learning acceptance frees you to set out on the path to real relationship wisdom. Remember that no one is perfect, and that both our faults and our lovable qualities make us the unique individuals we are.

Acceptance is the key to peace and harmony.

STEP TWENTY-SEVEN: RESOLVING CONFLICT: THE SOFTLY, SOFTLY APPROACH

Sometimes there are painful and difficult issues in a relationship which need to be discussed and sorted out, or problems that need solving. When something is troubling you or wrong in the relationship, one of you is probably going to bring it up at some stage, and the way in which you do this is crucial. All too often, the woman is the one who raises issues in relationships. It is a recognized fact that men are more fearful of discussing tensions and that women are better able to confront and deal with them. These gender-specific traits stem from evolutionary patterns, so it's best to work with, rather than resent, them.

HOW TO RAISE ISSUES IN A WAY THAT LEADS TO RESOLUTION RATHER THAN CONFLICT

Begin softly
Launching with a full-scale attack or an aggressive manner will switch your partner into defence mode and get you nowhere, so begin by appreciating your partner. For example, suppose the issue is that he is too distant and won't talk about his feelings. Begin by thanking him for his willingness to talk right now and to listen to what you have to say. Reaffirm your love and express how happy you are with him.

Talk about the problem using "I" statements
Sentences that focus on your feelings, such as "I feel frustrated and shut out when you won't talk to me about how you feel", are easier for your partner to listen to and accept, and they avoid casting blame in his direction.

Tell your partner what you would like
Be as specific as possible. For example, say: "I'd really like to know how you feel about us and whether you are happy with the way the relationship is going."

Keep the mood light
If the conversation get tricky, introduce humour and keep the tone affectionate.

Stop sooner rather than later
Even if you get a good response, don't push on to deal with ten other issues that have been causing conflict. Stop, give your partner a hug and get on with something else. If your partner stonewalls - that is, he refuses to respond or even disappears (for instance, behind a newspaper or computer) - STOP. This means your partner is feeling overwhelmed. Stonewalling is a stress response; it doesn't mean that he doesn't love you, but simply that he can't cope with the amount of information/emotion/volume coming his way. What may feel normal to you could feel huge to your partner. If you follow, badger or insist, he will disappear further for longer. So back off and wait for another time, then make your approach soft, warm and brief. Your partner will only respond when he feels safe and can actually listen to you without feeling, rightly or wrongly, that he is being ambushed.

Tread softly, and
solve difficult
issues successfully.

STEP TWENTY-EIGHT: NURTURING

To work successfully, a relationship needs nurturing. Just like a plant, it will grow stronger and thrive if it is treated with tenderness, fed and given the best possible advantages. In the early stages nurturing the relationship is easy. You are in love, the relationship is the centre of your life and there are few other demands. Later on other responsibilities can get in the way of nurturing it. Stress, exhaustion, work, children, health problems and financial pressures can all become major preoccupations.

Many divorced couples failed to nurture their relationship and then found that it had died. Often they realize, too late, that they didn't want to part and that there was so much to value in what they had together. When the relationship is in crisis, suddenly it becomes important again, and all other issues in life take a back seat. But by then it is so often too late: both partners are floundering and lost, with no idea of how to rekindle love and forge a new, even stronger union.

With love and effort, it is always possible to draw back from the brink. However, it is far better never to reach this point, and the way to ensure this is through nurturing.

HOW TO NURTURE YOUR PARTNER

Keep romance alive
In the early days, being romantic is easy, but later on it takes a little extra thought and effort. No matter how busy you are, make time to write a romantic note and leave it for your partner to find, or to buy a little gift or to plan a candlelit dinner.

Never take each other for granted
Couples become so used to one another that they can stop noticing little details. Look at your partner with fresh eyes, listen to what he says and notice the small changes. Has your partner put on a little weight, changed what he wears, begun frowning with worry more often? If you don't notice what's going on, you can't respond to it.

Make room for surprises
Life's day-to-day routine becomes dull and predictable, and that is why surprises are so wonderful. Present your partner with a weekend away, a special night out or a thoughtful gift.

Treasure the special parts of the relationship
At the beginning all couples have special activities that they enjoy sharing, but as time goes by these "luxuries" often disappear. Whatever your special things are - lingering baths together, passionate (not routine) sex, going for a walk or just talking - hang on to them (or enjoy finding new ones) and treat them as essential.

Be kind to each other
When one of you is sick, exhausted, disappointed, upset or feeling a failure, the other needs to be at his or her most sensitive and kind. Nurture your partner in whatever way he would most appreciate. Let him know that whatever goes on in the world outside, you will always love him just as much as before.

Remember that in order to nurture the relationship you need to nurture yourself, too, otherwise you will feel that you have nothing to give.

Nurture the love
you share and
watch it thrive.

STEP TWENTY-NINE: TREASURE WHAT YOU HAVE

Concentrate on feeling lucky - it's the best feeling in the world, so enjoy it! Switching your mindset from unlucky or down to lucky can be hard at times, but the effort it well worth it. The ability to treasure what you have in a relationship, and everything connected with it, is a wonderful gift and one that we all have. All it takes is a little willingness.

Often we focus on what is missing in our lives, and this applies to relationships, too. What are you unhappy or discontent about at the moment? What do you wish you had or want to change? Do you wish you had more money, that your partner would change in some way, that life were easier, better, simpler? Do you want to live somewhere else or be slimmer, sexier or funnier? Concentrating on what is missing or wrong is draining and requires a lot of energy, which could be far better used elsewhere. It often makes you ill and damages the relationship. It also gives the world the message that you feel discontent, and this will be fed back to you by the people around you. Remember that what you give out, you will attract. Make the decision today to be lucky and to treasure what you have.

HOW TO TREASURE YOUR RELATIONSHIP

Act happy
Smile, whether you feel like it or not, at everyone you meet and even smile when you're alone. It will convince your brain that you're happy, and then you will start to feel happy. Remember that feelings follow behaviour; behave as though you feel great and you will. Sing, dance, laugh and enjoy life.

See abundance everywhere
Your life is filled with love, successes and things to feel good about. Start to notice them.

Measure your progress
Give thanks for the ways in which you've both grown and adapted, and all that you've learnt together. A relationship makes you wiser.

Value your health
Studies have proved that couples in long-term relationships are generally healthier than single people, so glow with vigour and feel content.

Cultivate an attitude of gratitude
Give thanks for all you have. In bed at night, go over all the good things that have happened throughout the day.

Appreciate your partner
Think about his good qualities, talents and abilities, and see him as unique and special. Take delight in the fact that he has chosen to be with you and that you were wise enough to choose him.

Treasuring what you have is simply a new habit to learn. Like any habit, it requires repetition before you can do it without thinking. The same applies to feeling lucky. For the next two weeks, walk around telling yourself you are lucky and you can be certain that, before long, people will be saying: "You're so lucky, how do you do it?"

Treasure what you have, and attract more good luck into your life.

STEP THIRTY: CELEBRATE!

So, you've made it this far. Well done! Hopefully by now you are feeling optimistic about your relationship and the future. Whatever point you were at when you started this book, you should now be feeling better, stronger and more confident. Being in a relationship is one of life's richest blessings, and, if you love someone, there is nothing you can't resolve together. Working on the points raised in this book is way of investing in the relationship and acknowledging how important it is - that it's well worth the effort, time and trouble - and that's something to celebrate.

Congratulate yourself on getting this far and being willing to work on the relationship. Celebrate being with someone you care about so much and all the advances you've made. If you don't want to tell your partner exactly what the occasion is you're marking, simply say that you are rejoicing being with him, and that's cause enough.

Ways to celebrate your relationship:

* Do something different together or something familiar in a different setting - sex in the middle of the day, a picnic in the middle of the night or dinner in bed.

* Share a treat - perhaps a cake and a cup of coffee, or champagne and caviar.

* Have a night out enjoying a passionate opera, a romantic dinner or a sexy movie.

* Give each other a head-to-toe massage, with sensual aromatherapy oils and scented candles.

* Share a candlelit bath with bubbles, music and champagne.

* Cook dinner together, indulging in your favourite foods and plenty of legendary aphrodisiacs such as oysters and chocolate.

* Take a day off work just to be together.

* Shower your partner with romance - a sentimental card, a sexy present (and one for you), an early night . . .

* Surprise your partner - by kissing and making up sooner than usual after a fight, by giving in or by telling him that life's too short to argue.

* Take his breath away by paying special attention to the way you look.

Make this celebration the first of many, and don't limit yourself to just one from the above list - try them all! Celebrate every milestone you pass, no matter how small, making this a key feature of your journey through life together.

Celebrate the
pure joy of
being together.

A FINAL WORD

Whatever you do in life is worth doing to the absolute best of your ability, including being in a relationship. Why settle for ordinary, mundane, okay, passable, middling or bearable when you can have extraordinary, wonderful, exciting, satisfying, passionate and fabulous - the kind of relationship you deserve? The choice is yours, and you make it every single day that you stay in a relationship. Promise yourself each day that, if you decide to stay with this person, you will actively choose to have a marvellous life with your partner and to make the relationship as good as it can be.

Preventing the negative from overwhelming the positive will help the relationship become a balanced and fulfilling one that will last. Keep this in mind, always, and let it be your guide when making decisions. Resolve to limit conflict and pain and to nurture all that is good between you. Choose to notice and appreciate your partner, and opt for love and peace over hurt and fights. Enjoy to the full the fruits of your choices - greater love, peace and harmony.

NOTES